CONFESSIONS OF A MEGA CHURCH PASTOR

How I Discovered the Hidden Treasures of the Catholic Church

ALLEN HUNT

ISBN: 978-0-9841318-3-9

Nihil Obstat: Rev. Theodore R Book, S.L.L. 15 February, 2010

Imprimatur: + Most Rev. Wilton D. Gregory, S.L.D.,
Archbishop of Atlanta, 15 February 2010

The Nihil Obstat and Imprimatur are a declaration that a book or pamphlet is considered to be free from doctrinal and moral error. It is not implied that those who have granted the Nihil Obstat and Imprimatur agree with the contents, opinions, or statements expressed.

All Bible quotations and citations come from the NRSV CE – New Revised Standard Version, Catholic Edition, unless designated by a *, in which case the translation is my own. Any Bible quotations provided in **bold** letters indicate an emphasis that is entirely my own.

Peggy Noonan, John Paul the Great, Penguin Books, 2005

Joan Carrol Cruz, The Incorruptibles, Tan Books, 1977

Published by Beacon Publishing

TABLE OF CONTENTS

Dedicated with love to Anita.
Simply top drawer.

DAVID'S TALE

Twenty years ago, no one saw it coming. Not even David.

He was a young man working for a prestigious management consulting firm and he was in New York working on a project. Early one morning, David and a colleague jumped out of a cab and dashed through the freezing rain toward a Wall Street high rise, only to have to step over a homeless man who was sleeping in the doorway, blocking the entrance. David could not avoid facing the stark contrast of that scene.

Here he was, a young, slightly overconfident man, entering a monument to success and aspirations, and below him was an anonymous vulnerable human being trying to soak up the warmth coming through the grates from the subway down below.

David stopped in his tracks, and heard the Holy Spirit whisper in his ear. "When are you going to stop serving yourself and start serving me?"

That day David flew home and told his fiancée that the time had come. "I'm leaving the world of business to become a pastor."

For the next fifteen years, David's career would

blossom from one ministry to another, culminating in his dream job. He became the senior pastor of a mega-church, the most well-attended Methodist congregation in the South, and one of the largest in the country. Somewhere between four and five thousand people worshiped there each Sunday, listening to David preach. Eight thousand gathered there for Christmas and Easter services. The church sponsored one of just two K-12 Methodist schools in the nation, had a full pregnancy resource center, a counseling center, a child care ministry, and maintained partnerships with vital missions on every continent around the globe.

David had risen to what he considered the best position he could have in the Methodist Church in America. And then, twenty years after his first epiphany, he would have another, one that would be equally shocking and create deep conflict in David's life. It would stun his family. It would cost him a number of friendships. It would put an end to all he had worked for in his career as a pastor. And it would be impossible to avoid.

It culminated on Sunday, January 6, 2008, the feast of the Epiphany. David, the former pastor of a mega-church just twenty miles away, stood before the congregation at the Shrine of the Immaculate Conception, Atlanta's oldest Catholic church.

He was no longer the very public and well-respected Methodist minister. He would not welcome the congregation, deliver the homily, or stand outside and greet members as they left, but instead would be just like any other lay person there.

But then, finally, the moment came.

David walked to the front, and the priest gently placed the Body of Christ in the palm of David's hand for the very first time.

And David began to weep.

Tears slowly streamed down his face as the years of journey climaxed in the enveloping presence of the Holy Spirit.

During the twenty years since that fateful rainy day in New York City, God tested David's faith, challenged his health and overhauled His call to ministry. He revealed Himself to David in wonderful ways until David had no choice but to walk away from his generous salary, his small local celebrity and his job security. He would leave behind people he had loved deeply, and he would do so without the accompaniment of his family. David was that sure of God's calling him home to the Catholic Church.

In case you're wondering, yes, I am David, and this is my story.

How did my transition occur? Not in a single moment of great revelation, but slowly, through a series of experiences. More like a mosaic of God-encounters. Or better yet, like a journey on a boat that begins in the Atlantic Ocean, without a real plan or destination. One day you wake up, look around and realize that you're somewhere in the Pacific. You're not sure when you crossed from one ocean to the other, but you know you're there, and there's no going back.

Often, I was leading that wonderful mega-church, and deep inside I began to feel a longing to be a part of what I was convinced was God's One Church. Over time that longing grew until I could deny it no more.

How and why did this happen? In the pages that follow, you'll get the answers to those questions. In fact, you'll get six answers. Those are what I came to see are the six hidden treasures of the Catholic Church, treasures so powerful that they changed my life in ways I could never have imagined. And perhaps they'll change yours too.

I call them hidden treasures because they are so often over-looked or misunderstood or taken for granted. I've written this book for a variety of readers.

It is for those who, like me, have been curious about, or even had negative feelings toward, the Catholic Church. It is also for fallen-away Catholics who feel a yearning to rediscover the wonder and beauty of their Church. And it is for practicing Catholics who may have lost sight of what is right under their noses.

To demonstrate the hiddenness of the treasures of the Church, I'll use an analogy of an old house, and I will guide you through it and point out to you what I've discovered there. It is my prayer that, whoever you are, you'll discover in the walls of that house the beauty and truth and wonder that I did.

Most of all, I pray that the real-life recommendations I provide at the end of the book will give you real-life ways to experience the grace of God, and the treasures of the Church, for yourself. In providing these practical ideas, my hope is to offer life-giving insights for everyday living.

Finally, I should admit that writing this book has been difficult for me, because I share some of my deepest struggles and personal secrets. Not only do I make myself vulnerable in doing so, I could also risk someone misinterpreting my journey as a criticism of their own beliefs. Please know that this is never my intention. My hope is that by being honest about my own experience and conflicts and journey, others will be helped in similar ways. I write this book with great love. I love the Methodist Church, for it birthed my own faith in Jesus Christ. And I love the many persons who have shaped my journey from childhood and since those days when I stepped over that vulnerable homeless man in New York City.

But now that part of my journey is over, and I am finally home. What follows is what I have found in that home.

OLD HOUSE

...new treasures in all kinds of places.

"This house will take care of you." Those words rang in Steven's ears.

When he was just a little boy, Steven's father, Henry, walked him through the family home one day and said, "This house will take care of you. Everything you need is in this house."

Now, years later, Henry had died. Steven was now helping his mother pack up the family's belongings in order to sell the house and move to Florida to be near her grown children. As they walked through the house one last time, taking one final glance at the home built by Henry's own hands, memories flooded Steven's mind. And then came the words again, "This house will take care of you."

It was as if his father were standing right there to remind him. "Everything you need is in this house."

Henry had been a WWII hero, a Flying Tiger. Henry had radiated Yankee know-how, independence, frugality, and self-sufficiency. He had loved time in the woods. He had raised his children well, and he had raised them in that house. But now he was gone. Fifty years of memories had accumulated in that old house.

As Steven took that one last walk-through, he reminisced on years gone by, including his entire childhood and adolescence. He also looked for any possessions that might have been missed in the packing. In his parents' bedroom, Steven noticed an odd screw in the ceiling, an object that had never before captured his attention. Steven knew his dad's meticulous nature and assumed that the screw surely had some purpose, so he stepped up on a stool to look more carefully at the ceiling. When he removed the screw, a hidden panel emerged from the ceiling. Behind the panel rested two Folger's Coffee cans, each of which was filled with cash.

"This house will take care of you."

Steven's mind raced. If his father had hidden cash in one place, there might be other cans hidden as well. Steven soon discovered screws, hidden panels, and coffee cans all around that old house. Hidden treasures all around him, and he had never realized it.

By the end of the spontaneous scavenger hunt, Steven had found more than $5000, hidden years before in the old house by a Depression-era man who knew you cannot always trust forces outside your own house. In addition, Steven also found old report cards, children's notes and drawings, and other family memories his father had stashed away in those coffee cans. Instead of using safe deposit boxes, Henry had carefully hidden his treasure in the ceilings and walls of his own home. "Everything you need is in this house."

As you will soon learn, Steven played a crucial role in introducing me to Catholicism. Whether he intended to do so, I do not know. But it seems most fitting that his own father's story provides the metaphor for my simultaneously joyful and painful journey into the Church.

You see, for the first thirty years of my life, the Catholic Church was just an old house to me. An old house that often looked like it needed some sprucing up. To be sure, the Catholic Church and her history have not been without blemishes, and like any old house, the Church has a few creaky windows, a few cracks in the walls, and an occasional leak. Sadly, as an American and as a Protestant, I knew more about the blemishes than about the house itself.

Having grown up as a Methodist, having descended from at least five generations of Methodist pastors in the South, the Catholic Church existed in my world simply as an old house. The Catholic Church was old and historic, but it was never something that attracted my attention in any real way. Catholic churches were often physically beautiful, but I never really noticed anything else about the old house at all.

During my nearly twenty years as a Methodist pastor, I neither liked nor disliked the old house of the Catholic Church. In each town where my family lived, stood a Catholic church, which in my mind was just another church, one of the many varieties in the world. I really had no reason ever to notice its existence. I was not Catholic, nor was I particularly interested in those who were. It was just an old house, with some old rituals, old buildings, and old ideas. I paid it no attention.

Without my expecting and certainly without my invitation, God began to reveal to me irresistible treasures hidden in the walls of the old house known as the Catholic Church. In fact, as I moved through the old house, I discovered new treasures in all kinds of places. For example, in the dining room, I found the treasure of the real presence of Christ in the Eucharist. It had always been there, but it lay hidden in the wall. In the basement, I discovered a foot locker full of saints. In the bedroom, my wife shared the Church's mystery with me. Exploring the old house proved to be a thrilling and life-giving wonder in my life. In fact, the exploration proved life-changing. "This house will take care of you. Everything you need is in this house."

All in all, God showed me the treasures found only in the Catholic Church. He used them to paint a mosaic of truths and experiences in my spirit. As a result, after having served as an effective Methodist pastor for almost two decades, including the final eight years of my ministry at one of the largest Methodist congregations in the world, I left it all behind to enter the Catholic Church in January, 2008.

These treasures taught me that this old house is, in fact, my home. In these six treasures, I found life. A new home in an old house. A journey to the center of the heart of Jesus Christ and His intentions.

DINING ROOM

I began to crave the elements in my physical body.

The Catholic Church is mean. That was my first impression.

We were there for a funeral. My first visit ever to an actual Catholic church. While still attending seminary, I was serving as a Methodist pastor at a small church in rural Georgia. A close friend died. My wife, Anita, and I attended the funeral. So far, so good. Since I was a pastor, it just naturally occurred to me to stand and move toward the altar when the time came to receive communion from the priest. In the Methodist Church, the communion elements were offered to anyone who presents himself to receive. Moving forward was a natural response for me.

In the small church, with only a handful of pews, we were seated near the front, immediately behind the family of the deceased. When the priest issued the invitation at the funeral, I moved toward the aisle to go forward. As I stood, a woman directly in front of me, who knew me well enough to know I was not Catholic, turned around, stuck her finger in my chest, glared directly in my eyes, and said very pointedly, "*You* cannot receive communion *here*. Sit down."

Message sent. Message received. Clearly.

My takeaway? The Catholic Church is mean. At least that is what I thought and felt at the moment since this was my very first encounter in a Catholic church.

But years later, my experience in the dining room of the old house would change all that.

Sister Rose Plants the First Seed

Several years after that "sit down" encounter, the Holy Spirit introduced me to the dining room of the old house. It was there that God planted the first seed. I am still trying to understand how He did that. I do know this: it did not happen overnight. It was a gradual process, but when it did, the results overwhelmed me.

This dining room discovery was the very beginning of my journey home to the Church. Ironically, it also proved to be the final climax.

The dining room is where it began and ended. In a way, this makes sense. We often begin our family time gathered around the family table. We linger after meals in the dining room. For most families, our best conversations take place in the dining room. In more ways than one, the family table becomes the centerpiece of our family's life together. The dinner table cannot be replaced by the drive-through window nor by an entertainment center. Something mysterious, even sacred, occurs when we sit down together and break bread. Even research shows that families who eat together usually experience greater strength and remain together. It may be as simple as this: in the dining room, we share the family meal. And that meal binds us together.

In the same way, in the Catholic Church, the dining room takes center stage. It serves as the focal point of the entire house. Why? Because as a friend of mine says, "It all rides on the Eucharist." And it took me a long time to discover he is right.

After completing seminary at Emory University in Atlanta, my family and I moved to New Haven, Connecticut, for me to pursue a Ph. D. in New Testament and Ancient Christian Origins at Yale University. Of the four students admitted to the highly selective degree program that year, one was a Presbyterian, one a Jesuit, one a Dominican, and, of course, I was a Methodist. Much to my surprise, the Dominican friar, Fr. Steven, and I immediately became close friends upon meeting in our first week. Fr. Steven fascinated me. I had never spent more than five minutes with a priest in my life. He slowly opened all the doors to the Catholic Church for me. Up to that point, I really had had no exposure to the Church, but when it came, it came like water from a fire hydrant.

At times, God uses friendships in remarkable ways. We listen to real friends. To strangers, we often turn a deaf ear or a cold shoulder. But to real friends, we will listen, even when listening stretches us in new ways. I do not think Fr. Steven intended to lead me home. Rather, he loved me and my family with abundance in a time when we desperately needed it. That friendship and love led to conversations about things of faith. Those conversations percolated and bounced around in my soul for years. I am constantly amazed at how God uses genuine friendships to shape our lives.

Essentially what Fr. Steven did was he introduced me to the dining room and the family meal. In our second year together, Fr. Steven arranged for the two of us to give Lenten lectures to a group of cloistered Dominican nuns in North Guilford, Connecticut. Of course, first, he had to explain what a cloistered monastery was. Talk about naive! I had no idea such places even existed.

A gathering of 50 nuns, located in a monastery whose grounds they vowed never to leave. A place of regular prayer, Mass, and simple, humble service. A group of nuns who supported their mutual life of prayer by making fudge (and it was great fudge!) and operating a book store. It was in their monastery that God planted the first seeds for my conversion, seeds which took sixteen years to come to fruition, and seeds which I did not even realize were being planted at the time.

Fr. Steven and I spent four wonderful afternoons giving talks to the nuns at the Monastery of Our Lady of Grace. I discovered later that I had been the first male who was not an ordained Catholic priest ever to instruct the sisters within their walls. It was a rare privilege and blessing, which I could not have fully appreciated at the moment. God had opened a door of grace into which I had stumbled.

Best of all, the experience proved eye-opening for me in more ways than one. This invitation into a cloistered monastery rocked my world.

The holiness of these sisters stunned me. Keep in mind that these women would be the first to disagree at any suggestion that they are holy. They would be wrong.

Never before had I encountered persons so completely given over to God. Their faces shone with a grace and a light that unnerved me. The love of God revealed itself physically in their eyes, cheeks, and smiles. These were women whose entire lives were dedicated to the glory of God.

Remember this was totally new to me. I had no context or background to understand this place or these women. No such group exists in any Protestant tradition. Very simply, I was bumfuddled. It is not often that we have an experience that is so out of the ordinary and so out of place that we have no real way to process it at first.

This was all new territory to me. In some ways, it was scary because I was accustomed to teaching, speaking and being in charge of my setting. That control and leadership clearly did not apply here.

Fr. Steven and I shared lectures focused on the great Dominican doctor of the Church, Thomas Aquinas, and on John Wesley, the founder of the Methodist movement. We discussed sanctification and holiness, and the places where our beliefs intersected far more than we had anticipated. The common ground between us surprised the nuns, Fr. Steven, and me. We enjoyed great interaction and conversation together. After our last lecture, we reserved time for questions and answers. For many of the sisters, I was the first Methodist they had ever met.

One sister, whom I call "Sr. Rose," raised her hand and, as I remember, said, "Allen, thank you for having come these past few weeks. We've enjoyed your teaching." She paused and continued, "You sound so Catholic. After hearing you, I can't help but wonder, 'Why aren't you a part of the Church?'"

The nuns giggled. The question startled me. "A part of the Church?" What did she mean? As a Protestant I was taken aback by that. I thought to myself, "Well, I am a part of the Church. Don't you understand that? I'm a Methodist pastor." Then all of a sudden it dawned on me: she meant the Catholic Church is the one and only Church.

I laughed and gave a quick answer. I said something like, "Why am I Methodist as opposed to being Catholic? Well, you are some of the first Catholics I have ever met. The main reason revolves around communion. It seems very obvious to me that Jesus is using a metaphor when He talks about the cup and the loaf. The wine doesn't literally become His blood; that seems kind of obvious to me as a Methodist. It's still wine, or in the Methodist tradition, it's grape juice. The loaf, He is saying, 'It's my body,' just as He also says He is the door, He is the light, and He is the shepherd. It's just bread and juice. I really do not understand why you all take it so literally. It's a symbol."

Believe it or not, I had never had that conversation in my brain before. As a Methodist and in my training in seminary, it was just something we assumed. I took it for granted.

Sr. Rose then came right back at me. Very kindly but very directly, she said, "Well, you are a New Testament scholar, right? So why does Jesus say..."

With that introduction, she then began to walk me through chapter 6 of the Gospel of John and Jesus' teaching there on the Bread of Life. I thought I knew this passage, but Sr. Rose carefully paused on eight separate occasions to make the point: Jesus is serious about His body and His blood.

6:35: *I am the **bread of life**. Whoever comes to me will never be hungry, and whoever believes in me will never be thirsty.*

6:47: *Very truly, I tell you, whoever believes has eternal life. I am the **bread of life**.*

6:51: *I am the **living bread** that came down from heaven. **Whoever eats of this bread will live forever**; and the bread that I will give for the life of the world is my flesh.*

6:53: *So Jesus said to them, "Very truly, I tell you, unless you **eat the flesh of the Son of Man, and drink His blood**, you have no life in you."*

6:54: *Those who **eat my flesh and drink my blood** have eternal life, and I will raise them up on the last day; for my flesh is true food and my blood is true drink.*

6:56: ***Those who eat my flesh and drink my blood** abide in me, and I in them.*

6:57: *Just as the living Father sent me, and I live because of the Father, so **whoever eats me will live** because of me.*

6:58: *This is the bread that came down from heaven, not like that which your ancestors ate, and they died. But the **one who eats this bread will live forever**.*

To be honest, the whole situation was a bit embarrassing. My lack of training and preparation became obvious. As Methodists, we rarely talked about what we believed was taking place when we shared communion. I had never really questioned whether anything was taking place at all. It was just a symbol, which meant it was not very important to us.

Ironically, years later, when I sat on the large committee of Methodists who would decide which candidates for full-time ministry would be ordained, our group had frequent discussions about whether a candidate really understood "the sacraments." On occasion, I would suggest to that group that *none* of us had any idea what the sacraments, particularly communion, were about. That is why we were Protestants in general, and Methodists in particular. Sacraments were helpful, but they were hardly central to our Protestant faith. It was those Catholics who focused on and valued the sacraments, not us. Eventually, that recognition in my own spirit created a chasm I could not bridge. I was serving as a Methodist pastor in a Church who really had no idea what they believed about the sacraments.

Back to Sister Rose. Here I was, an ordained Methodist pastor, being schooled by a very kind, very direct Dominican nun. *I* had been invited to instruct *them*, and now *they* were instructing *me*. The irony was obvious.

What I had always read as merely a very repetitious chapter of Jesus instructing the masses, Sr. Rose revealed as the very essence of the Church. For me, communion was mildly interesting; for her, the Eucharist was life.

However, Sr. Rose was not done. She then moved on to 1 Corinthians 11 and pointed out how the apostle Paul uses the same language of Jesus,

> *For I received from the Lord what I also handed on to you, that the Lord Jesus on the night when He was betrayed took a loaf of bread, and when He had given thanks, He broke it and said, "**This is my body** that is for you. Do this in remembrance of me." In the same way, He took the cup also, after supper, saying, "**This cup is the new covenant in my blood. Do this, as often as you drink it in remembrance of me**." For as often as you eat this bread and drink the cup, you proclaim the Lord's death until He comes.* (1 Cor. 11:23-27)

"*This is my body...this is my blood.*" Sr. Rose instructed me. Her teacher for the past few weeks became her student for five very awkward minutes. In front of the whole group, she said, "It doesn't say this is *like* my body. It doesn't say this is a *representation* or *symbol* of my body, or this is kind of a symbol of my blood. It says this *is* my body and this cup *is* my blood. What don't you get? Allen, what do you not understand?"

We all laughed, I shrugged it off, and we moved on. However, as kind and gentle as she had been, she had made her point.

I did not realize it at the time, nor did I understand it until years later. However, that seed, carefully planted by the Holy Spirit through Sr. Rose, eventually led to my conversion.

Dining Room Centerpiece

God continued to water that seed, often in unseen ways. Only years later, did I notice the verses that follow Jesus' instruction on the Bread of Life in John 6. In looking back at the end of that passage, I noticed John 6:60-66, where many followers fall away because of the difficulty of Jesus' teaching on the Bread of Life. People abandoned Jesus because His teaching on the Eucharist was "too hard." They were offended, even disgusted, by the image of His being the body and the blood.

Why would people abandon Jesus if He were only using the Bread of Life as a metaphor? That makes no sense. Clearly, they were offended at the idea that they would eat the body of Jesus and drink His blood.

In a recent estimate, the *World Christian Encyclopedia* suggests there are more than 33,000 different varieties of protestant Christianity, and among those 33,000, there are thousands of views of what's happening in the Eucharist. Many small independent congregations each have their own unique beliefs about the Lord's Supper. Baptists see communion as merely remembering what Jesus did way back then. Methodists say Jesus is especially present, more so than at other times, but only spiritually so. How did we arrive at so many different understandings of the Eucharist when, for the Church's first fifteen centuries, Christians shared unanimity about this? Where did all this division over communion come from? And how could this possibly please God?

The language describing the mystery of the Eucharist in the New Testament, upon which all Protestants seek to base their beliefs, is amazingly consistent. The same terms and ideas occur not just in Matthew, Mark, and Luke, but they transcend those similar gospels even into the Gospel of John and then into the letters of Paul. Nearly all the writers of the New Testament address the Eucharist, and they all do so with consistent terms and language. Writers who had little or no access to each other or to one another's writings, use nearly identical words and phrases when addressing the Eucharist.

The New Testament is clearly consistent. The real presence of Jesus in the Eucharist is important.

We are accustomed to Matthew, Mark and Luke sounding the same. They often use identical language for Jesus on many things. So it is not surprising that they do so regarding the body and blood. Take a look at Luke 22:19-20.

> *Then He took a loaf of bread, and when He had given thanks, He broke it and gave it to them, saying,* **"This is my body, which is given for you.** *Do this in remembrance of me." And He did the same with the cup after supper, saying, "This cup that is poured out for you is* **the new covenant in my blood.**"

Notice how strikingly similar the words of Jesus

in Luke are to what the Apostle Paul says in the 1st Corinthians passage above, the passage used by Sr. Rose to remind me of this basic lesson.

And the same can be said for another Gospel, Matthew 26:26-28:

> *While they were eating, Jesus took a loaf of bread, and after blessing it He broke it, gave it to the disciples, and said, "Take, eat;* **this is my body**.*" Then He took a cup, and after giving thanks He gave it to them, saying, "Drink from it, all of you; for* **this is my blood** *of the covenant, which is poured out for many for the forgiveness of sins."*

And for Mark 14:22-24.

> *While they were eating, He took a loaf of bread, and after blessing it He broke it, gave it to them, and said, "Take;* **this is my body**.*" Then He took a cup, and after giving thanks He gave it to them, and all of them drank from it. He said to them, "***This is my blood*** *of the covenant, which is poured out for many."*

Why does this matter? Remember that the apostle Paul did not have the Gospels, and the Gospel writers did not have Paul. The Gospel writers may not even have had each other's words to compare, and the Apostle Paul almost never makes references to the words of Jesus in his letters. However, when it comes to the Eucharist, the Apostle Paul uses nearly identical language to what Jesus Himself says in Matthew, Mark and Luke. This similarity simply does not occur on any other topic. Ever.

Not only does Paul describe the Eucharist, he does so in language just like that of the first three Gospel writers. That Eucharistic language must have been really important in the early Church. Everyone was speaking the same language.

Moreover, John is a world unto himself. His Gospel is totally unlike the other Gospels. Yet, again, he uses the same language they do on one key topic: the Eucharist. How can this be? Very simple. The early believers all spoke the same language when it came to the focal point of their faith, the Eucharist.

Virtually no other words of Jesus in the gospels are replicated, almost verbatim, word for word, in the letters of Paul. Yet Paul's phrasing matches that of the gospel writers too. Somehow I had also missed that important fact in all my studies and in all my preparation.

In other words, there is more uniformity of language in the key New Testament writers regarding the Eucharist and Jesus' words about His body and blood than on any other topic. Multiple writers, all composing their works in different places and at different times, and usually without access to one another, consistently share the exact same language about the presence of Jesus in the Eucharist. They do not show this kind of consistency on any other subject. Why would that be? Because the Eucharist is so vital, so central, so important.

Sr. Rose helped me begin to think about what really happens when we share the body and blood. Her spontaneous question eventually forced me to begin considering, even though it took many years, how Jesus is fully present in the Eucharist. I began to struggle with why my own Protestant experience focused so much on the sermon and the pastor while early Christian worship focused so much on the Eucharist.

This discovery did not occur in an instant for me. In fact, the struggle was very painful. Words cannot describe the internal conflict I felt in my final months as a Methodist pastor when celebrating the Lord's Supper. Here I was, leading thousands of people to the table of Christ, and deep within me, I was struggling with what really was taking place on that altar. I knew something more was occurring. After all, early martyrs had been willing to die so as not to compromise their convictions about the presence of Christ in the Eucharist.

On what grounds did I explain the elements of communion? Whose opinion did I trust? Scripture? If so, those elements really are the body and blood of Jesus. Church tradition? If so, those elements for the Church's first fifteen centuries were unanimously declared to be the body and blood of Jesus. Where did I get this idea that Jesus was merely "especially present" and that was it?

This internal conflict was painful. As hard as it is to admit, I felt something like a fraud. I no longer believed in what I was doing. What an awful feeling – to be in your dream role at a wonderful church with ministries spanning the globe and to know deep down that you have an integrity problem.

As I discovered the central place the Eucharist has played, and therefore can and should play, in the

Church, my soul began percolating: I had no idea why I was separated from the Church founded by Jesus and His Eucharist. As a Protestant, I had no idea what I was protesting.

Crazy Yearning

God was drawing me to Himself. It was just taking me time to figure it out. When my family and I vacationed, I chose to worship at a Catholic church, an unusual habit for a Methodist pastor. Since I was a Protestant pastor, I always wanted to be sure to go to worship on vacation since those Sundays were precious occasions when I did not have the responsibility of leading worship.

Let's be honest. In the Protestant experience, it all rides on the sermon. By going to a Catholic church, I knew exactly what I would be getting. The worship would not be focused on the sermon, the preacher, or the music; it would be focused on the altar and on the Eucharist. If the message was good, that would be great. If the music was rich, that would be just fine too. But that really was not the point. The point is the Eucharist.

After vacations, I grew increasingly uncomfortable with the emphasis on the pastor's sermon as the centerpiece of worship in the Protestant church. My soul wrestled with how my brothers and sisters would identify their churches by the pastor's names. "We go to Pastor Bob's church." "We attend Dr. Johnson's church." "We have a dynamic young pastor." It all felt so superficial and personality-centered.

Again, too often everything hinged either on "I liked the sermon," or on "I did not like the sermon." My ego might swell when a new arrival in our church would say, "I am here because I just love your preaching." And my ego might fall when I would receive an email from a church member telling me that they were "shopping for a new church" because my preaching just did not "feed" them. Either way, swollen or fallen ego, my soul always knew that the sermon as centerpiece just felt wrong. Surely there was more to the Church than that.

By contrast, in the Catholic Church, worship revolved around the altar and the family meal, the Eucharist. The Mass focused on the holy gift of God as He comes to us in the precious body and blood of Jesus.

Since I was unable to receive communion in the Catholic Church, I merely sat and marveled at the beauty and the majesty of the Mass. The holiness enveloped me. My spirit exalted at the new world opening before me. My eyes watched as others went up to receive the elements.

Eventually, I began to yearn to receive the elements with my fellow believers. This feeling cannot be captured in words.

First my spirit began to yearn to share communion with other believers. Then my body literally began to cry out for the body and blood of Jesus. I craved the elements in my physical body. I know it sounds crazy. But no other words do it justice. A deep spiritual craving, then a physical one.

These were new dimensions of faith. Having

physical cravings for the body and blood of Jesus in communion was not only a new experience for me, it was also a shocking one.

God was drawing me like a metal shaving to a magnet, and I no longer had control of the direction. I had visited the dining room, and now I was struggling to get my footing. My body was craving to eat from the table.

Adoring the Straw

The final piece fell into place in the chapel of a Catholic church near my home. I had no idea what this chapel was: an *adoration* chapel. Like my time with the cloistered nuns, where I knew nothing of a cloistered monastery, again I knew absolutely nothing about adoration. Perpetual adoration. My training had never even mentioned such a thing.

Spending time and reflection in front of the blessed Sacrament, merely pondering the mystery of Jesus' gift to us and His presence with us. What in the world was that?

In its little adoration chapel, this church offered Masses at 6:45 am and 9:00 am each weekday. I began to attend and sit in the back in order to mind my own business, and not get in the way of people who were doing things that were utterly foreign to me. I felt simultaneously completely at home and completely out of place.

Bizarre. A trained, ordained Methodist pastor, with a Ph.D., and I had absolutely no idea what these people were doing. At the end of the Mass, they brought out the monstrance (yet another something I had never seen or heard of before). It is extraordinary. Each day, they placed it there on the altar, and the believers knelt and prayed before it. Perpetual adoration. Twenty-four hours a day, seven days a week in this tiny chapel. This odd habit fascinated me. I found myself mesmerized. Time spent merely gazing and pondering the mystery of the Eucharist and Jesus' gift in it.

God's magnetic attraction continued. I began showing up every so often, not knowing what adoration was, but being attracted to it in spite of my ignorance and participating in it in my own imperfect, meager way. Really, what I was discovering was God's drawing me to Himself through His self-giving love there on the altar. This small chapel became a source of new clarity. I observed other believers in adoration, gazing at the sacrament and at the crucifix hanging above it. My eyes landed on the beauty of the sacrament and the message it conveyed: Jesus comes to us. He is a gift. He feeds our souls.

It became obvious why Catholics had built such beautiful cathedrals and churches throughout the world. Not as gathering or meeting places for Christians. But as a home for Jesus Himself in the Blessed Sacrament. Cathedrals house Jesus. Christians merely come and visit Him. The cathedrals and churches architecturally prepare our souls for the beauty of the Eucharist.

One day, as I sat in the back of that tiny chapel, the priest shared the experience of St. Thomas Aquinas. A brilliant man, and one of the most prolific writers the Church has ever known. Yet, as Aquinas celebrated Mass on December 6, 1273, for the Feast of St. Nicholas, he became utterly dumbstruck with awe by what happens in the elements, their transubstantiation into the body and blood of Jesus. He was so overcome that he simply sat down and could not finish the Mass. Speechless.

Aquinas, the brilliant scholar, later wrote, "All that I have written seems to me like straw compared to what has now been revealed to me." One of the Church's greatest thinkers overwhelmed by the real presence of Jesus in the Eucharist.

Eventually, in that chapel, deep in my heart, I knew. Sister Rose was right. God offers Himself to you and me in the blessed body and blood. It really is true. So I quietly prayed, "Lord, forgive my unbelief." This sacrament really is what Jesus said it is. The real presence of Jesus among us. It all rides on the Eucharist.

The Eucharist is our family meal. It is the gift of God. Jesus comes to us and feeds us with Himself in the elements. Our worship focuses on the altar because that is how and where Jesus presents Himself to us.

The Eucharist also binds us together. Without the presence of Jesus in the Eucharist, we merely have our own ideas rather than true unity. In the Eucharist, Jesus fuels and empowers His Church. Everything rides on the Eucharist.

Very simply, God changed my heart.

"This house will take care of you. Everything you need is in this house."

KITCHEN

At age 89, Father Caj had been wounded in prayer.

Suffering changes things.

Unfortunately, I learned that lesson from life rather than from a book. However, through my suffering, the Holy Spirit revealed to me the second treasure. And I found it in the kitchen of this old house.

Wounded in Prayer

Great storms often arrive when you are not expecting them. When our family moved to Connecticut for me to attend Yale, on the day we moved, our older daughter, SarahAnn, turned two years old, and our younger daughter, Griffin, had only been with us for six short weeks. Little did our family know that great tests lay ahead. And also great rewards.

Anita and I were nervous about many things. Nervous about how we could afford this venture as a family of four. Nervous about what lay on the other side of the degree – whether it be teaching, preaching, or something else. Nervous about leaving our home in Georgia to move to New England, a thousand miles away. Nervous about being young parents with small children, living so far away without the immediate help of our families. Nervous about whether I could perform at the level that would be required to earn this degree. Nervous.

God was teaching us trust. And He had only just begun.

Within a week of arriving at Yale, my health collapsed. The doctor diagnosed ulcerative colitis, and for the next two years, we desperately tried anything and everything known to control the symptoms and the disease. The battle included regular trips to the hospital, and the loss of control of my bodily functions. The doctors tried experimental treatments and diets while my health got worse and worse. My weight dropped from 155 pounds to 128 pounds, and my body became stooped and pale.

Because of my illness, our three years in New Haven produced suffering and struggle. Each day, my life was governed by pain and by having to know where every bathroom was located. Before stepping out of the house each morning, I thought through every building and every walkway my day would include so that my mind could anticipate where bathrooms were located in the event of an emergency.

Embarrassing accidents became the norm on occasions when I frantically needed a bathroom. In a parking lot. On the side of the road. In the park. The good news was these embarrassments certainly created lots of opportunities to grow in humility!

The doctors prescribed steroids to ease the pain and to help my colon, but the steroids slowly transformed my personality into a more volatile, short-tempered one. I became less and less of a pleasure to live with. My wife was not only raising two small daughters, she now was also taking care of an increasingly frail and temperamental husband.

To make matters worse, for the first time in my life, I was at the bottom of my class. Of the four students admitted that year to Yale's intense and competitive doctoral program, I clearly was the most poorly prepared. For the first time in my life, I was not at the top of the heap. In fact, it was obvious to everyone that I was at the bottom. Suffering health. Struggling performance. Strain on the family. Tough times.

My poor preparation revealed itself most plainly in our coursework in classical Greek, the original language of the New Testament. In Greek, I struggled mightily, performed poorly, and worried greatly. My ability to remain in the graduate program hinged on my passing this class.

My good friend, Fr. Steven, was far better prepared than I was. In order to get assistance, I made a near-daily stop by the priory community of priests where he lived on my walk home from classes. He could offer coaching to help me with Greek.

When I stopped by the priory, I entered through the rear door, which led into the kitchen. I chatted with the cook, Mary, until Fr. Steven came downstairs to work with me at the kitchen table.

Upon entering the kitchen, I was usually met by

Fr. Cajetan Sheehan, a Dominican friar like Fr. Steven. Retired, Fr. Caj was 89 years old when I first met him. He stood about 5'2" and weighed perhaps 120 lbs. A wisp of a man with clear eyes and a fiery spirit.

Fr. Caj had "retired" from more than a half-century of pastoring parishes and had evolved into a new ministry of prayer. Each morning and each evening, he and the other priests in the priory gathered for prayer. While some priests attended as they could, Fr. Caj *always* attended. He lived for prayer.

Without fail, each time that I saw him, Fr. Caj asked about my health because he knew I was suffering. He asked about my wife and children since Fr. Caj knew they were having a hard time. Every time he saw me, he would say in his curmudgeonly New England Catholic priest kind of way, "Well, I've been praying for you."

I knew those were not empty words. Prayer saturated Fr. Caj's life. If he said he was praying, our little family knew he meant every word of it.

When he retired, the secretary at his new home, St. Mary's Priory, always knew that if someone in the parish needed a pastor in an emergency, Fr. Caj was the one to call. He stood ever ready and eager to assist a person in need at any hour of the day. Even at age 89, Fr. Caj stood ready to do the right thing rather than merely the convenient thing. His was a retirement from pastoring but not from full-time service. Not only did Fr. Caj devote himself to prayer, he poured himself out generously at all hours of the day.

When I met him, Fr. Caj was still wearing the same clothes he had been wearing for nearly thirty years. He saw no need for new ones since the old ones worked just fine. He placed all of his small pension each month in the Poor Box, where believers could give to ease the hurts of people in need. In his mind, the parish where he lived already provided all that he actually needed. His room, his meals, and his toiletries. Fr. Caj figured that was enough. So he gave away all that he had.

Generous giving. Compassionate service. And a life devoted to prayer. At age 89, Fr. Caj was something to behold.

One day, I stopped by the kitchen and ran into Fr. Caj. His appearance startled me. His head was swollen with a bandaged, large bruise on his forehead.

"Fr. Caj, what happened?" I asked.

His matter-of-fact reply came, "Oh, I was in the prayer chapel, and I was praying for you. And I fell asleep and hit my head on the railing. So I went to the hospital and got this."

He bowed up with just a touch of pride in his face to display the bandage in all its glory. The first time I had ever seen someone with a red badge of prayer courage! At age 89, Fr. Caj had been wounded in prayer.

In this diminutive man, I encountered a deep holiness that comes only with time and experience. Different from the gentle holiness of the nuns I had encountered, Fr. Caj's holiness was a rugged holiness (if there is such a thing). A holiness refined by decades as a priest in every imaginable setting. Years of faithfulness and testing.

I use the image of the kitchen here for holiness in a different way from the other rooms of the house, so please be patient with me. But the experience of meeting Fr. Caj in that kitchen so many times made a significant impact on me. His impact was so great that I have linked the treasure of holiness to the kitchen even though the connection is not so obvious.

If you met him, the truth was obvious: Fr. Caj and Jesus were good friends. The Holy Spirit flowed so deeply in Fr. Caj's veins that holiness nearly oozed out of his pores. That holiness never landed him on any magazine cover nor did it ever make him wealthy. It just made him a whole lot like Jesus.

Why had I never encountered this level of holiness before?

I knew a lot *about* holiness. But I had never *met* holiness like I experienced personally in Fr. Caj Sheehan in the kitchen of St. Mary's Priory.

The Holiness Factor

As a Methodist, I certainly knew *about* holiness. It was the whole reason Methodism existed in the first place. John Wesley built the Methodist movement in England to help followers to grow in holiness. He developed a "method" for holiness. Believers used these methodical practices to become more and more like Christ.

Over time, Wesley's insistence on "method" (where the term "Methodist" comes from) has slowly been lost in the Methodist Church. We rarely talked about holiness or the means to pursue it.

When I was teaching a class for new members, a man raised his hand and asked me, "Where does the term 'Methodist' come from?"

I explained about John Wesley and his "method" for becoming holy. The man asked if Methodists still use that method. I replied that we no longer really had a common method even though we were Methodists.

He then asked, "Then what is a Methodist *now*?"

Embarrassed, I had no response.

We Methodists had very little doctrine in common, and we rarely utilized the actual teaching of John Wesley anymore. The Methodist Church was focused on other things now. Here I was - a prominent Methodist pastor who had no idea what a Methodist even was anymore.

Now back to Connecticut. My battle with ulcerative colitis came to a climax after two years of suffering. We had tried everything, every experimental treatment, steroids, and all kinds of dietary restrictions. Nothing had worked.

I lived on high doses of steroids for the disease, and those drugs affected not only my body but also my temper. My life was becoming nearly unmanageable.

After two years of deterioration, I asked for surgery. Anita and I consulted a surgeon who pointed out that surgery would provide a cure - a radical cure, but a cure nonetheless.

Finally, I had my large intestines, my colon, entirely removed.

The good news: no more colitis.

The bad news: I would wear a bag on my mid-section for the rest of my life.

Sadly, in this same period of time, Anita also suffered two painful miscarriages. At one time, we were actually both in the same hospital together, she for a miscarriage procedure and I to have my colon removed.

As a result of Anita's health issues, our plans for a larger family would not materialize. Shortly after the removal of my colon, I was then diagnosed with the deadly cancer, melanoma. Since it was detected early, I did not require chemotherapy or radiation, only minor surgery.

Clearly, as a newly married couple, with two small girls, we were suffering. The strain was real. Our relationship and our family was being forged deeply in a crucible of suffering.

We could not see what was happening at the time, but God was slowly drawing us to Himself in a way we had not experienced before. He was also preparing us for what lay ahead in our lives and ministry. If we could withstand this suffering, we could face nearly anything

Radical surgery. Two miscarriages. Melanoma. 1000 miles from home. The end of dreams for more children. Struggling with rigorous studies. All within two years. Needless to say, we were shell-shocked.

But we were still standing. And the rugged, holy prayers of Fr. Caj fed our souls like manna in the desert.

Fr. Caj prayed for us each day. He bathed our lives in grace, often without our knowing it. His prayers and the prayers of the Dominican sisters carried us through a period of suffering and led us closer to the heart of God.

Your Holiness Destiny

Holiness matters because holiness is your destiny. God makes that clear.

God's will for your life becomes clear in 1st Thessalonians 5:23-24 when the apostle Paul writes,

*May God himself, the God of peace, **sanctify you through and through**. May your whole spirit, soul and body be kept blameless at the coming of our Lord Jesus Christ. The one who calls you is faithful and **He will do it.***

God intends to make you holy. In fact, that is His will for your life. You are destined for holiness. The only question is whether you will cooperate with His intention now or wait for Him to make you holy later.

This short letter, 1st Thessalonians, is warm and affectionate. The Apostle Paul shares his genuine affection for the Thessalonian people because he started this church. This letter displays Paul as the caring pastor.

The first half of the letter expresses Paul's love and concern while the second half instructs them on being prepared for the return of Jesus. Since Jesus is coming soon, believers get ready by focusing on holiness.

In chapter 4, Paul coaches them (and us) on how to live.

> *Finally, brothers and sisters, we ask and urge you in the Lord Jesus that, as you learned from us **how you ought to live and to please God** (as, in fact, you are doing), you should do so more and more.* (4:1)

It is important not merely that we think rightly but also that we behave and live rightly. To please God.

Then in 5:15, Paul summarizes of how we are called to behave.

> **See that none of you repays evil for evil, but always seek to do good to one another and to all.** *(5:15)*

The message of 1st Thessalonians is so simple:
I love you.
I give thanks for you.
Jesus is coming, so please God rather than yourselves.
God wants you to be holy.
Holiness means not repaying evil with evil, but seeking to do good.
Put the pieces together, and you arrive at the climax of the letter: the destiny of holiness.

> *May God Himself, the God of peace, **sanctify you through and through**. May **your whole spirit, soul and body** be kept blameless at the coming of our Lord*

*Jesus Christ. The one who calls you is faithful and **He will do it.** (5:23-24)*

Live to please God, and He will make you holy. He will *sanctify* you (make you holy) through and through. He wants to make every part of you holy. Without that, you will never enter into His presence.

Best of all, God *will* do it because He is faithful. He does what He says He will do.

Do you get it? Paul is making sure they are prepared for the coming of the Lord.

To make his point, Paul gives a prayer at the end of each half of the letter. The first prayer calls for love to abound so we can grow in holiness.

*Now may our God and Father Himself and our Lord Jesus direct our way to you. And **may the Lord make you increase and abound in love for one another and for all**, just as we abound in love for you. And **may He so strengthen your hearts in holiness** that you may be blameless before our God and Father at the **coming of our Lord Jesus** with all His saints. (3:11-13)*

Wow, those are three marvelous verses.

Paul links how they live *now* with what will happen when Jesus returns. We need to be prepared. We are on a venture, a journey of holiness, and this life is not a dress rehearsal. We are preparing for God by becoming holy and blameless.

Then, at the very end of the letter, Paul writes what may be the best prayer of the entire New Testament. This eye-popping prayer closes the entire letter.

*May God Himself, the God of peace, **sanctify you through and through**. May your **whole spirit, soul and body be kept blameless** at the coming of our Lord Jesus Christ. The one who calls you is faithful and **He will do it**. (5:23-24)*

God will make you holy, which means that you will look like Jesus. That is your destiny. God keeps His promises and will do what He says. It is not a matter of *if*, but only a matter of *when*.

These two powerful prayers (3:13-14 and 5:23-24) reveal the treasure of holiness. One word captures 1st Thessalonians.....*holiness*.

So what does holiness look like? Remember that, Saint Paul connects holiness to love. Holiness and love go hand-in-hand. There is no holiness apart from love.

Jesus taught us to 1) *Love* God and 2) *Love* People. The Eucharist embodies the love God has for us as He gives Himself completely to us. That love flows and brings the holy character of God into you. Then, there is love for one another and for all people in the believing community as well as love for those outside the community. So holiness is a huge package of love that allows God to make our hearts flawless. This is what we were made for: holiness saturated with love.

Perhaps the easiest way to remember this is by memorizing a little tiny half-verse in 1st Thessalonians 4:3.

*For **this is the will of God, your sanctification**:*

If you have ever worried, "I wonder what God's

will for my life is," the answer is simple: holiness. It is also easy to forget. *His* will for *your* life is your sanctification, your *holiness*. That clears things up, doesn't it? You are called to holiness. That may mean that you are a nun or a lawyer. You may be a mother or a single professional. But God's will for your life is the same: holiness, no matter who you are. *That* is why we are created. We are created to be holy in love, in love with God, in love with other people, and in love with the community of believers. That's what we are all destined for - holiness in love.

When you suffer, you are being conformed to the image of Jesus. When you pray, you are being made holy in the image of Jesus. When you quietly serve a person in need, you are being shaped into the image of Jesus. When you generously give, your heart is being remade into the image of Jesus, our Lord and Savior.

This is great stuff. Your destiny is holiness. You will look like Jesus through and through. Only then will you enter the throne room of God. And everything you do to seek Him or to please Him grows you one step forward in His image. One step closer to your destiny of total holiness.

Best of all, in 1st Thessalonians 5:24: *God will do it*.

What a relief! It's not you and I that produce holiness. We are called to be holy. We are striving to be holy, but God produces and generates the holiness. The holiness comes from Him not from us. We merely cooperate with God. You were made for holiness, and God keeps His promises.

An Alzheimer's Habit

Now, as Fr. Caj was praying for our family, we also were introduced to Sister Diane. She led the community of Dominican nuns, the group I mentioned in chapter 1 regarding the Eucharist.

Each time I instructed the nuns at their cloister, Anita and our girls would play in the cloister yard and wait for our time to conclude because they were not allowed behind the cloister wall. In her gentle, caring way, Sr. Diane would greet them and receive them with warmth. She baked homemade cookies on every visit so our girls would know they were welcome and expected. Sr. Diane would spend time with Anita to communicate how the sisters loved us and were praying for us during our time of struggle. In one word, she was delightful. God's grace literally leaped from her cheeks and emanated from her eyes.

Fifteen years after that first time I spoke to the nuns, I returned after my conversion to Catholicism to share lectures with them once more. This return engagement brought things full circle. We had been together when I was first introduced to the old house of the Church, and now some 15 years later, I had fully moved into the house. Then, I had been sick and our daughters were pre-schoolers. Now, I was well, and our girls were preparing for college. Sadly, in the years in-between, Sister Diane had died.

For the last years of her life, Sr. Diane had experienced the slow deterioration of Alzheimer's. As a member of a cloistered community, she never left the monastery grounds. Her sisters cared for her. Each step of the way, each day, they loved her into death and into the loving arms of Jesus.

As her Alzheimer's progressed, Sr. Diane would wander the property each day, always carrying with her a copy of *The Wellsprings of Worship* by Corbon. This marvelous little book describes the Mass as the river of life for our souls. While she was healthy, Sr. Diane had loved this book, having read it dozens of times in her years as a sister. The book reminded her each time of why she had entered the monastery to devote herself fully to our Lord.

Even with Alzheimer's, as she was losing her faculties a little more each day, she treasured that book and carried it with her everywhere she went. As her sisters prayed throughout the day, Sr. Diane would sit in her familiar place in the community, flipping through the pages of the little book about being drawn into the life of God. She could no longer comprehend the words she read, but the words nourished her soul nonetheless. It was as if she knew what she was reading in spite of her mental loss.

In other words, Sr. Diane had developed a habit of holiness when she was alert, and that same habit became so deeply engrained in her DNA that it continued all the way to the end of her life. Even when she could not consciously choose to do it, the habit persisted. What she had done when she had all her wits about her, she continued to do even in her Alzheimer's confusion because prayer and worship had become the defining part of who she was. Devotion to God was not something Sr. Diane *did*. Devotion to God defined who she *was*.

You begin to pray, you make time for worship, and

eventually you develop a habit that leads you closer and closer to holiness. In doing so, slowly, almost imperceptibly, over time, you become holy. Holiness is your destiny if only you will cooperate with God. Best of all, He will make you into what He intended for you to be in the first place. The best version of yourself.

What a marvelous image. When all else around us fails, still there is God and still there is worship. Sr. Diane was so conformed to the image of God, so attached to the liturgy of the Mass, that she and Jesus had become one. In contrast to Fr. Caj's curmudgeonly, rugged holiness, Sr. Diane displayed a radiant, elegant holiness.

Holiness is so palpable and prevalent in the Catholic Church because God comes to us in the Eucharist and the altar with the very gift of Himself, His body and blood. Through that offering on the altar, God then infuses us with His holiness and with His grace in the body and blood of Christ.

Over time, day in and day out, prayer, devotion and the Mass have an overwhelming effect in our lives. They produce holiness.

A Drink of Holiness

As a Methodist, the Pope was irrelevant to me. With the election of John Paul II, that all changed.

For some reason, I paid attention to this little Polish man who seemed so loving. Like so many other pieces of God's mosaic in my soul, I cannot explain how the Pope's holiness attracted me. Holiness emanated from Pope John Paul II, even through a television screen. Thousands of people appear on television, and not a single one communicates holiness. Yet, John Paul II merely passed by in his vehicle, waved, or spoke a word to the crowd, and a gentle holiness emerged from the television. How could holiness translate through a television screen?

His holiness attracted me like a thirsty man to a glass of cool water.

One word describes John Paul II: *different*. Of course, John Paul II lived a life devoted to continuous prayer. Spending time in adoration before the Blessed Sacrament was a staple for his day. Seeking complete resonance with God.

Peggy Noonan's account (*John Paul the Great*) of the events of May 13, 1981, captures the essence of Pope John Paul II.

It is 1981, and John Paul II has been pope for about two and one-half years. He arrives in St. Peter's Square at 5:00 pm in the afternoon among a crowd of nearly 20,000 people. The Pope smiles, waves, holds children, and he blesses them. It is a marvelous day.

Suddenly, a shot rings out; then another. Shots from an automatic pistol as a Turkish prison escapee, a Muslim man named Mehmet Ali Agca, attempts to assassinate Pope John Paul II. One bullet grazes the Holy Father's elbow. The second bullet pierces his side and enters through his abdomen. He falls backward, into the arms of his personal secretary, Fr. Stanislaw Dziwisz.

Those around the Pope say the Holy Father immediately began to pray. In other words, the Pope's very first impulse in a crisis is to speak with God and to pray. Just as Sister Diane had developed such an engrained life of continuous prayer that her devotion continued even into her decline into Alzheimer's, the Pope so embodied prayer that he continued devotion even into the valley of the shadow of death. A prayer reflex.

Those nearest him sense that he will die. The bleeding is profuse, and the damage great. As he prays, the Pope realizes it is 5:00 pm. on May 13. He has the presence of mind to remember that, on this day in 1917, the virgin Mary first appeared to the shepherd children in the field near Fatima. So, of course, the Holy Father begins to pray to Our Lady of Fatima.

Keep in mind that the Pope has five internal abdominal wounds and the primary bullet has missed his main abdominal artery by $1/10^{th}$ of an inch. Even in that distressing moment, John Paul II has the presence of mind to recognize that sixty-four years before, something momentous had occurred.

So the Holy Father prays to the Blessed Mother for help.

At five o'clock in the afternoon, the trip from St. Peter's Square to the hospital, because of traffic, averages thirty minutes. That day it takes just eight. The Pope spends five hours in surgery. Everyone just knows he is going to die because the damage to his body is so horrific. Yet, John Paul II said later, "I had a vision that I was going to be saved."

The Pope comes out of surgery, and what is the

first thing he does? He asks to see the bullet. They bring him the assassin's bullet that surgeons have removed from his body. He rolls it around in his fingers and instructs his staff to take the bullet to Fatima and have it grafted there into the crown on the statue of our Our Lady.

The Holy Father realizes he has never met or expressed forgiveness to his assailant, Mehmet Ali Agca. So the Pope, the head of the Church, goes during Christmas week to Rebibia, the death row prison in Italy, to meet personally with Agca.

John Paul II, in his person, brings all these strands of holiness together. Paul instructs the Thessalonians (5:15), "*See that none of you repay evil for evil, but always seek to do good to one another and to all.*"

Before their meeting, the Pope celebrates Mass with the death row inmates. Afterward, the man who occupies the seat of Peter sits for two hours in plastic chairs with the man who tried to end his life. The two men sit directly across from each other, the Holy Father and the murderer who tried to kill him.

As they meet, the Holy Father discovers that Agca is mortally terrified of the Virgin Mary. Agca reasons that since Mary had saved the Pope, she would then kill Agca for his crime. For two hours, John Paul II shares grace and love with a Turkish Muslim prison escapee. He explains to Agca that the Blessed Mother loves him and yearns for him to know her son, Jesus. Two men sitting in one of the darkest places on earth, death row, and for a moment, an intense concentration of the light of Christ fills the room.

From that moment, the Pope and his assailant shared a bond. In 2005, when the Holy Father lay dying in the hospital, he received a get well card from Mehmet Ali Agca. When the Pope later died, the first request the Vatican received to attend the funeral Mass was from Agca as well.

The Pope had such impact not because of what he did, but simply because he was. Holiness in prayer and devotion, in forgiveness and love.

That is our destiny. You and I are called to holiness.

Holiness resides in this old house, God's Church. The same holiness that resided in Father Caj, and in Sister Diane, is the same holiness that emanated from John Paul II like a magnetic force field. That holiness originates on the altar of the Church where Jesus feeds us with His own body and His own blood.

Through my many encounters with Fr. Caj in the kitchen, I met holiness. And along the way, I discovered our destiny: Holiness.

After all, "Everything you need is in this house."

BASEMENT

What exactly am I protesting?

Scary things live in the basement. Families even hide their secrets in the basement. But the basement also provides the foundation for the house itself. No foundation, no house.

Big Opha's Basement

When my grandmother, Opha, died, my brother and I found a treasure chest.

Opha had lived in the same house for over sixty years, a four room house near the Ohio River. This little ninety-five pound, blue-eyed, lady possessed remarkable courage and strength. In her eighties, she still picked up and drove her circle of "old women" to church, even though she was the oldest member of the group. She lived by herself for decades after my grandfather's death. And she loved me uncondition-ally for all the days she knew me.

When Opha died, my mom, who is an only child, asked my brother, James, and me to clean out the storage shed in the back yard. Grandmother's shed served as her basement. The small space was filled with yard tools and boxes of stuff. Opha liked to save things. From old dolls, to letters written by my mother, to newspaper clippings highlighting the exploits of her beloved Cincinnati Reds. Opha's basement was filled to the brim.

In her basement, James and I found a large foot locker, looking eerily like a treasure chest. We had never noticed it while we were growing up. Then again, given all my grandmother's stuff, it was easy to miss.

The foot locker was locked, but as we shook it, we could tell it was full of stuff. Perplexed that a treasure chest would have sat there unnoticed all those years, James and I grew curious. We had no idea what we might find inside.

My mind began to run wild. We had discovered a locked, previously unknown foot locker, hidden away in mounds of stuff. Inside were possessions of my beloved grandmother who clearly must have been squirreling away important valuables! My mind flashed with the possibility of a hidden pirate's treasure that my grandmother had stored for years and never revealed to anyone. Or a collection of bejeweled family heirlooms that she had never mentioned even to her own daughter. A treasure of jewels and gold to be discovered only after her death, a secret known heretofore only to her. I could see it in my mind's eye: this treasure would make our family rich beyond our wildest imaginations and dreams!

And it did.

My brother and I pried open the treasure chest with a screwdriver, eagerly anticipating the riches soon to be pouring through our fingers. As we opened the foot locker, we discovered it was filled to the brim with......old pictures. Old, black and white photos. Thousands of them.

Photos of all kinds of people in all kinds of poses. Photos of people from an era long since past. Long beards and mustaches. Long dresses. Wagons. Horses. Farm people.

These photos captured the faces of my grandmother's family members and friends who had filled her life with joy. But, even though we knew these people must be related to us, we had no idea who any of them were. We only knew they were important to my grandmother. Why else would she have kept their pictures?

We sifted through the old photos like precious gems, and then turned them over, looking for a written message on the photo's back describing who was captured in each shot. Sadly, they contained no writing or identification whatsoever.

Here we were, in possession of thousands of photos of people who were important to us (because they were important to our beloved grandmother), but we had no clue who these people actually were.

What a tragedy! These people were part of my family, yet I had no idea who any of them were. They had lived in the basement all these years. In fact, over the previous century, they had provided the foundation for my grandmother's life just as she had done for my own. But their stories and significance were completely lost to us.

In a way, it was like being an orphan. You know you have relatives. You must have them because you are a human being. But you just are not sure who they are or where they are from. You know nothing about the rich stories of their lives and your own heritage.

Instead of being connected to those who had gone before us, these family members were completely lost to us. In a sense, we were orphaned from our own family.

As a Protestant, I found the saints to be just like these old photos in the basement. I knew that the saints existed. After all, names like Francis, Thomas, and Catherine occasionally showed up in literature. But I certainly did not consider them my own *family*.

The saints were Catholic, and I was not. They had lived and died a long time ago, and I knew almost nothing about them. How could they possibly have anything to do with me? I possessed no connection to these people.

I had recited the Apostle's Creed for most of my life, professing my belief in the "communion of saints," but I had no idea what that "communion of saints" actually meant. I certainly had never believed that I was a part of these saints' family and that they surrounded me and were encouraging me forward in faith toward Christ. They were just dead people from the past. They were not my family.

Until I met John Fisher.

Head on a Bridge Post

John Fisher. Became Bishop John Fisher. Then Cardinal John Fisher. And finally St. John Fisher. In doing so, he paid a very high price.

In 1529, King Henry was making preparations to get rid of his wife, Catherine of Aragon, in order to replace her with Anne Boleyn, while John Fisher served as the bishop of Rochester. Fisher and a number of other bishops defended Catherine both publicly and vigorously against King Henry, and Fisher even worked on Catherine's behalf in Parliament, saying that he was willing to die on behalf of the sanctity of marriage.

Because of his public support for Catherine from 1529 to 1535, King Henry made John Fisher's life a living hell. Fisher lost his property and possessions. He suffered intense persecution and torture, experienced public humiliation and ridicule, and spent countless months in extreme isolation.

In 1530, the authorities arrested John Fisher for the first time. They tried to poison him, but the attempt failed. In 1532, not only did John Fisher stand in the way of Henry's marital divorce from Catherine, he also opposed Henry's move to divorce the English Church from the Mother Church in Rome. In doing so, Fisher blocked Henry's plot to place himself at the head of the English Church as king.

In 1534, John Fisher was thrown in prison again. The King confiscated all of John Fisher's property as well as his freedom. The losses had only just begun.

In 1535, Pope Paul III intervened to help John Fisher, so he named Fisher the Cardinal Priest of St.

Vitalis. By doing so, the Pope hoped to demonstrate authority and support for Fisher in the face of Henry's persecution. The Pope believed that an elevated office for John Fisher would keep him safe from the king's violence.

In fact, just the opposite occurred. King Henry told the Pope there would be no need to send the cardinal's hat to London for Fisher; Henry would simply send the new cardinal's head to Rome instead.

Henry then placed John Fisher in the Tower of London, and sentenced him to death. Executioners beheaded him.

The soldiers threw Fisher's naked body into a grave, then took his head, and placed it on a pole on London Bridge. Henry left it there for two weeks for the public to see just how serious he was about being the head of the Church in England. Fisher's face continued to radiate such a ruddy look that the soldiers finally removed it and threw it into the Thames, replacing it with Thomas More's head instead as a continuing reminder of what would happen to those who opposed Henry.

In the nearly 500 years since Cardinal John Fisher's death, the Catholic Church each year has requested access to the small chapel in the Tower of London where Fisher worshiped and prayed as he awaited his own execution. The Church hopes to celebrate a Mass on the date of his martyrdom. Each time, the Church's request has been denied.

Believe it or not, I first heard about John Fisher when I was attending the World Methodist Conference in England. The conference sought to bring together several thousand people, to celebrate the hundreds of varieties of Methodist Christians, all of whom considered themselves spiritual descendants of John Wesley.

On the trip, Anita and I visited English holy sites like St. Paul's Cathedral, Westminster Abbey, and Canterbury. Along the way, we learned of the English martyrs. King Henry did not like the Truth so he established his own truth. A truth where he was free to shed one wife for another at his own pleasure. A truth where he would replace the Pope and serve at the helm of the church in England. Henry disagreed with the Church, so he created his own. He then commanded everyone under his reign to follow suit, or else. Fifty-four priests, including St. John Fisher and St. Thomas More, stood in his way. So King Henry killed them all.

As I heard the stories in England, my mind bubbled. My own Methodist Church stood directly in the lineage of the Church of England, started by King Henry for less than seemly reasons. Once Henry's initial rebellions set church conflict into motion, the resulting energy spun off (and continues to spin) into all directions and forms. Over time, each new church or movement, borne of some conflict or another, stakes out its own claim to truth. Each new group defines itself in opposition to the group from which it spun off.

The obvious hit me: the authority for the English Church ultimately resided in King Henry's zipper and not in the Church.

The Methodist Church had always been an assumption for me. My family had been saturated in Methodism for generations. My relatives had launched Methodist colleges, edited Methodist newspapers, unified Methodist denominations, and led Methodist congregations. Still, I had never seriously considered the origin and authority of my own spiritual home. Until I met John Fisher on that trip to England.

John Fisher served me up with a crisis of conscience. Here were some of my spiritual ancestors, including John Fisher and Thomas More, standing for Truth and dying in the process. The depth of their convictions startled me. More and Fisher believed so deeply in the sanctity of marriage, and in the authority of the Church's teachings, that they were willing to suffer and die.

I asked myself: do I believe anything so deeply that I would be willing to stand for it in the face of great persecution? Fisher and More stood not only for their own faith but for the Church. What would cause men like Fisher and More to forfeit their possessions and their lives when their faith in Jesus was not being questioned, only their loyalty to the Church?

Did I have any deep convictions whatsoever about the Church of Jesus Christ? Honestly, the answer was no. That answer disturbed me.

Of course, the Catholic Church was not without fault in the 16th century. But the King of England simply severed England from the Church altogether, and installed himself as the new head of a separate Church.

On what authority? His own.

On what grounds? His lustful desire for a new wife.

To what ultimate end? This calamity provided the basis for the Church in which I presently lived and served. I was standing on shaky ground.

No wonder our little global gathering of a variety of Methodists in England could not agree on what Methodists were or what we believed. Not only were we not bound together by the real presence of Christ in the Eucharist, we were not bound together by any common authority at all. Like the example of Henry, we were following the example of every man for himself.

This left me with an unsettled feeling, which is not something you just walk up to your Methodist bishop, or your fellow pastors, and discuss.

Do you just approach your Methodist bishop, "By what authority do you lead? On whose authority do we stand? Do we have a really good reason not to be a part of the One Church founded by Jesus?"

How do you say that you are having a crisis of conscience?

A lot of my colleagues thought I was crazy when I did begin to have the conversation. So I usually avoided it. One Methodist denominational leader told me, "Allen, you think too much."

More comically, after I had converted and had been Catholic for a year and a half, I was invited to speak at a nearby Catholic parish for their Lenten mission. Over four nights, I shared some of the inspiring treasures of Catholicism but was struck by one comment from a staff member who lived near some of my former Methodist parishioners. Most of the Methodists I know have been very gracious to me in this transition. But when this Catholic staff member mentioned that I would be speaking at their parish, one of the members of the Methodist church I had led looked shocked and said, "Why would you invite him? He's crazy." The staff member and I shared a good chuckle together. Following God's leading does not always win you friends. In fact, it may cost you a few.

In these questions, you can hear the irony, can't you? Here I was, a prominent leader in the Methodist Church with no idea what Methodists actually believe.

Remember in chapter 1, when Sister Rose asked me, "Why are you not a part of the Church?"

Then, I had laughed off the question and dismissed it when she had asked it. Now, the question haunted me. St. John Fisher had forced me to confront something I couldn't shake.

I had met my spiritual ancestors in the basement of the old house, and their stories raised questions. Questions I should have, but never had, considered before. Questions like: Why is the body of Christ so divided? Does all this division bring pleasure to God? Do we Methodists really have a special reason to exist or are we just another splinter group refusing to acknowledge Church authority and Truth?

St. John Fisher had much to protest. He stood between Truth and error, willingly defending Truth at any cost. His strong stance raised questions for me about the validity of the Church of England and the Methodist movement in its origins and its authority.

Finally, I asked myself a basic question. Do I have a good reason to be separated from the Church and the Truth or am I just in rebellion out of convenience or pride?

I could find no justifiable reason to be separated from the Church. I remembered a quote from Fr. Richard John Neuhaus: "The only alternative to obedience is the cacophony of human beings making it up as they go." Neuhaus had converted from Lutheranism once he became convinced that Protestants were merely making it up as they go. Now, I faced the same crisis of conscience as Neuhaus. Would I have the courage and nerve to stand with the Church or would I remain Protestant simply because it was easy? Or because my pension depended on it?

Your Philippians Family

The Apostle Paul writes his letter to the Philippians from jail. Nestled right in the middle of this marvelous little letter lies an important description of the treasure of the saints, our spiritual family. To understand it completely, we need to get a quick snapshot of the letter of joy, the letter to the Philippians.

My friend, Craig Wansink, has investigated Roman prisons and written the definitive work describing life in a Roman prison in the first century, where survival usually meant living beneath the ground, in cave-like settings with little or no lighting. There was no such thing as private quarters, and in most cases, men and women were thrown in the same space together to fend for themselves. Worse, the gases from any candles or flames used to attempt to light the cave made the air toxic. Prisoners often went stir crazy and lost their minds.

As a prisoner, your ability to survive hinged on friends who would stop by and lower food down into the cave for you (and any others who got to it before you did). Fortunately, the Apostle Paul had reliable friends because of his faith. The Church literally fed the Apostle Paul.

All in all, life in a first century Roman prison could be described as dismal, dank, dark, and desperate. Prisons were places of death. The words used to describe ancient prisons were the very same words used by early Christians to describe hell. That's what prison was like - hell.

It is remarkable that, from the most dismal and dank circumstances imaginable, Paul writes Philippians. Miraculous and wondrous, really. In Philippians, Paul writes a letter of joy and thanksgiving to dear friends who have supported him not only in his mission but also in his imprisonment.

In Philippians, we possess the most joyful, grace-filled letter of the Bible, yet it was written from the most hellish place on earth.

In spite of his circumstances, Paul's heart bursts with warm affection for this special group of people.

I thank my God every time I remember you, con-

stantly praying with joy in every one of my prayers for all of you, because of your sharing in the gospel from the first day until now. I am confident of this, that the one who began a good work among you will bring it to completion by the day of Jesus Christ. (1:3-5)

With an understanding of the circumstances Paul faces in prison, we receive a lesson on the treasure of God's family, the saints. At the end of chapter 3, Paul writes these words.

*Brothers and sisters, join in imitating me, and observe those who live according to the example you have in us. For **many live as enemies of the cross of Christ;** I have often told you of them, and now I tell you even with tears. **Their end is destruction; their god is the belly;** and their glory is in their shame; **their minds are set on earthly things.***

But our citizenship is in heaven, and it is from there that we are expecting a Savior, the Lord Jesus Christ. He will transform the body of our humiliation that it may be conformed to the body of His glory, by the power that also enables Him to make all things subject to Himself. (3:17-21)

The crucial word in this passage is a little word: "But." There is one way of living, *but* then there is our way of living as Christ-followers. Everything hinges on that word, "but."

Paul describes the enemies of the cross of Christ. They focus their earthly lives on earthly things. They seek fine meals, precious jewels, earthly possessions, and pleasures of the flesh. In the end, they come to destruction.

But. But those who follow Jesus seek a different path. *Our* citizenship is in heaven. *We* pursue transformation by the power of Jesus, and His resurrection of glory. He has been raised. He will raise *us* too because we belong to Him, not to the world.

In other words, you and I are part of the colony of heaven. Right now, we may reside here on earth, but our passport indicates that our citizenship is in heaven. We are *on* the earth, but not *of* the earth. We are not fully at home here. We certainly pursue God's passions and desires of justice, peace, love, and grace as His people. *But*, in the end, we know that our citizenship really is not here.

You and I are yoked because our citizenship is in heaven from where we await the Savior, Jesus Christ. By the way, this is the only time in all of his letters that St. Paul ever uses the word "Savior" to describe Jesus.

Why would Paul only describe Jesus as "Savior" when reminding us of our heavenly citizenship? The Apostle Paul wants to help us avoid the confusion of thinking that our Savior comes from a government or any earthly figure. Our Savior is not a president, a celebrity, or some political leader. Those persons are mere earthly dwellers just as we are. In contrast, the people of God have a glorious Savior, a one of a kind Savior. Jesus.

We belong to the Church, to the family of God. Our family lives in heaven. Our deepest allegiance is to that family, our Savior's family. As important as our earthly families may be, in the end, we will arrive in heaven, the land of our home.

Our home is not a house here on earth. Our home is with God. Our family is with Him. He is the Father of our family, and the saints surround Him.

Your Spiritual Cheerleaders

Now imagine that you are a college football player for a major university, like the University of Michigan. On game day, you dress out in your full uniform, in the classic maize and blue. You wear pads to protect yourself from harm and harsh hits, and you place your Wolverine helmet on your head to keep you safe from the opponent. You hold hands with your teammates as you prepare to run from the locker room into the tunnel leading you out into the packed stadium, the nationally renowned "Big House." As your feet hit the turf, the largest crowd in America, with more than 100,000 fans, stands, screams, cheers, and sings to encourage you. The band plays "Hail to the Victors" at full blast.

Many of the alumni who have attended the university before you fill the seats. The fans, the band, and your teammates are Wolverines. You are family alongside them. The Wolverine family. They want you to win. They consider themselves part of your team even though their time at the university has already come and gone. You are a part of a team who is encouraged by a huge team of fans not only in the stadium but also watching on televisions in bars and homes and listening on radios in cars and trucks all over the country. Wolverines everywhere are watching you and cheering you on.

In the same way, you are a member of the family of God, the Church. Each time you walk into church for Mass, the saints surround you. Your family stands and urges you onward toward the altar and the real presence of Jesus.

Not only on Sundays, but each day, as you get dressed in your uniform of the day, you are ready to enter the world for work, for school, or for other assignments. As you enter the world each day, you spiritually are holding hands with your teammates, your fellow believers. Now note this: as you run out into the world, countless fans cheer you on, all the saints and believers who have gone before you. They are on your side. They want you to win. And they are watching and cheering.

The writer of Hebrews makes it clear at the beginning of chapter 12.

> *Therefore,* **since we are surrounded by so great a cloud of witnesses,** *let us also lay aside every weight and the sin that clings so closely, and* **let us run with perseverance the race that is set before us, looking to Jesus the pioneer and perfecter of our faith,** *who for the sake of the joy that was set before Him endured the cross, disregarding its shame, and has taken his seat at the right hand of the throne of God.*

As believers, you and I are running a race. Life is a journey, and we are headed toward our home with God in the Kingdom. The colony of heaven.

We run this race in a stadium surrounded by a

great cloud of witnesses, the communion of saints. They have run the race before us. St. John Fisher, St. Catherine of Siena, St. Rita of Cascia, St. Thomas Aquinas. They cheer us on.

And we are all looking toward Jesus, the pioneer and perfecter of our faith. He went first and is now at the throne of God. We follow Him and that line of saints who have gone before us and now cheer us onward from the stands.

Remember this - when you go to Mass, you are not alone. Look around you in the church. Remember your fellow believers are on the same journey you are. Then, look in the rafters, the niches, and the environment around you; look carefully. Most churches will have statues, stained glass windows, or icons of believers and saints who have gone before you. They are not there merely for decoration. They help you see your spiritual family all around you. They serve as reminders that you are not alone.

You are surrounded by your spiritual family. They do not need to remain in the basement. The saints are there, encouraging you, praying for you, supporting you, and cheering you on. Like a crowd on its feet to cheer you as you rush into the stadium, your fellow believers want you to finish the race well. They are the communion of saints, and they are very much alive. You can know their names, and you can learn their stories. You can even invite them to pray for you. Remember this - they are *for* you!

As a Protestant, I had no memory and no family. Until I met St. John Fisher, I thought I was on my own. It was just me and Jesus trying to run this race. Through John Fisher, God introduced me to my family, my teammates, and my encouragers. Then I realized: I am not alone, and neither are you. We are a part of a great family.

Since I have converted, my Protestant brothers and sisters insist on reminding me, "We don't worship the saints, Allen, we don't worship the saints."

Of course, we do not worship the saints.

Then again, neither do we ignore them. They are our brothers and sisters. They sit in the arena and cheer for us, and they are on our team. They have done what we hope to do.

Why would we ignore people who want us to succeed? They are our family.

Why would we not want all of our family to pray for us? We are not orphans with unknown ancestors. We know our family, and they know us. We are surrounded by a great cloud of witnesses who help us follow Jesus.

Would you want to run the race by yourself? Of course not. You and I don't pray to the saints. We pray *with* the saints. We invite them to pray with us. It is a remarkable privilege. They give us extra strength. They help us. Just look at Revelation 5:6.

> ...*the twenty-four elders fell before the Lamb, each holding a harp and* **golden bowls full of incense, which are the prayers of the saints.**

Do you see it? Before the very throne of God are twenty-four elders, each of whom holds a golden bowl filled with the prayers of the saints. Seated in the center of heaven is God the Father Himself, with Christ the Lamb at His side. Right before God are the prayers of the saints. Those prayers emit a pleasing fragrance into the nostrils of God.

Imagine that: our spiritual teammates and family are praying for us. Their prayers are incense in the nostrils of God. They are right there – in front of Him. Praying for you and for me. Why would you not want that?

We are not alone.

Your Family Welcomes You Home

Atlanta houses the busiest airport in America. It's gargantuan, and it is awful. When your plane lands in Atlanta, you get off and walk one or two hundred yards down a concourse to go down an escalator to get on a tram. The tram travels beneath the multiple runways and eventually stops at the terminal and baggage claim area. When you get off the tram, you step onto a huge escalator to take you up to the street level to claim your bags and meet your ground transportation.

I have never seen an escalator anywhere else remotely the size of this one. It's probably four stories, and it just goes and goes and goes. When you come to the top of that escalator, you choose either to go left or to go right for your baggage depending on your airline.

At the top of the escalator stands the waiting area. This is the closest that anyone who is waiting to meet your arrival in Atlanta can get to you. They stand at the top of that steep four-story escalator and wait for you to arrive.

In that waiting area stand chauffeurs and drivers with little signs that say "John Smith" or "Johnson Party." Greeters stand with signs, with balloons, and with eager faces teeming with anticipation. Children stand and wait for mom to come home from a long trip. Mothers wait for their soldiers to come home. The USO volunteers lead cheers each time a soldier pops up at the top of the escalator. Eyes sparkle with eagerness as if to say, "A special person is about to arrive, and we are here to greet them!"

They stand waiting and peering at the top of the escalator as each passenger pops into view.

"Will the next one be our family member?"

"Is that him?"

"Isn't she supposed to be here by now?"

The waiting area tingles with delight. Each passenger arrives to squeals of joy, roars of laughter, streams of tears, bear hug embraces, and twirlings around in the arms of family.

Every possible emotion lives in that waiting area. Excitement electrifies. Joy greets the arrival of a long-lost friend. Sadness embraces a family member who is arriving for a funeral. At any moment, several hundred people stand in the waiting area looking for that one person who means so much to them.

I imagine heaven works in the same way. Each of us arrives into the presence of God, appearing on the horizon like travelers from a faraway land. We pop up one at a time, travelers emerging at the top of a rising escalator. Our family members and "heavenly greeting team" stand waiting, tingling with delight and joy as they anticipate our arrival. One day, you and I are going to come up a very large escalator into the smiles, tears, and embraces of a heavenly welcoming committee.

Greeters will burst with joy when someone arrives from below. When you come up the escalator, you will hear wonderful words like, "Oh, we're so glad you're here. Welcome home. We have a place here just for you. Well done!"

That's what it will be like to be a part of the family.

Just in case God asks who I want to be there, I've got my list ready. My desired greeting team includes not only my father and grandmother, but also John Fisher and John Paul II, Teresa of Avila and Catherine of Siena, Fr. Caj, Sr. Rose, Sr. Diane, Blessed Mary, and Jesus Himself. All waiting to receive me as the newest arrival into the family of God once and for all. Waiting to say, "Welcome home!"

The Eucharist generates holiness, and holiness creates the saints I found in the basement of this old house. Now I know their names and am connected to my heavenly, eternal family.

"This house will take care of you. Everything you need is in this house."

BEDROOM

*Anita and I had met the mystery
of God in our own bedroom*

Some people sneeze from hay fever. The world
sneezes at mystery.

We live in a world where many people believe
they can explain everything.

"Jesus did not walk on water," they say. "He merely
stepped in shallow places."

"God did not create the earth or the universe; a
huge collision of matter simply exploded and the
world came into existence."

"Humans do not see visions; their brains fire neurons in a different way that creates the illusion of a
supernatural vision."

"Angels are not real," and the list goes on and on.

But you and I know better. The world may be allergic to mystery, but we are not.

My Wife, the Mystic

Anita and I met while we were in college. I noticed her our first year there; she still insists that she had no idea who I was until our third year (you can believe whomever you wish!). We began dating in earnest after graduation when we were both working in Atlanta. As much as her physical beauty attracted me, Anita's spiritual beauty and her firm sense of who she is attracted me even more. In fact, they still do. I knew after only a few dates that she was the woman I wanted to spend the rest of my life with.

Anita loves children and has a passion for helping them learn how to read. I admire that. Her love for family and her love for God have shaped me greatly, so it is not surprising that using her strong family background as a Southern Baptist, Anita re-introduced me to my own faith.

I had taken a hiatus from my faith life for a number of years, but when we began dating, Anita insisted that I attend church with her. She made it clear. Church was important to her, and if I was going to be important to her, church would need to be important to me. Crystal clear.

After a few dates, I knew she was going to be important to me, so I offered a compromise. I just could not see myself in a Baptist church, so I suggested we attend a Methodist church together. She agreed. I then suggested that we attend an early morning service so that I could use the rest of my day on other things rather than having the whole day taken up by church. Obviously, at the time, I was more interested in Anita than in my faith!

God bless her. Anita went out and found a Methodist church near her apartment, so I could pick her up early in the morning on a Sunday in order to go to a nearby church. On our first visit together to worship in that Methodist church, I knew I had been away for too long. Faith in Christ was my center, and I had wandered away from that center. Through Anita, I had rediscovered it.

When we married, I was not aware of Anita's rare gift. She has the characteristics of a mystic even though she is very uncomfortable with it, and we do not discuss it much.

On several occasions over the past 30 years, she has received visions or dreams from God. One or two have been easily discerned, but we do not always understand them at first.

This gift of receiving visions is not an easy one to have or receive. For every dream or vision received from God, at some point, Anita also has a chilling encounter with Satan and evil. In other words, they seem to alternate. A divine dream may occur, and then before the next one arrives some years later, Anita will have a terrifying dream or sense of the overwhelming presence of evil around her. We still work at discerning this gift together, and we also prepare ourselves for the assault of evil on occasion.

After a recent vision, she awakened me in bed with a question: "Do you think I should share this with Rhonda?"

When I asked what she meant, she then shared what she had just seen.

Rhonda's father, James, passed away several years ago. We had not known him well, but we had met him in person a few times. He was a big figure, larger than life. Standing physically tall in stature, James also had possessed a large personality. People loved him wherever he went. He was the center of attention and the life of the party. Since his death, James' wife, Rose, had missed him terribly, and their family had been struggling with a number of challenges including one daughter (Rhonda's sister, Lisa) who was dying of cancer.

In her dream, Anita had seen James and his wife, Rose, but not as the elderly adults we had known. Rather, they were in their early 50's in the vision, and the setting clearly was on the Florida coast. Anita saw James standing across from a sliding glass door that peered out onto the beach, much like he was in a hotel room or condominium. In his hands, he held a checklist with a number of things on it.

In the dream, Anita sat on the bed next to her own mother, and said, "Do you see him?" Her mother responded, "Yes."

Behind James, through the window, sat Rose, on a dock or pier with her feet dangling in the water. Her smile consumed her face. She was joyously happy.

As James looked happily at Rose through the glass, he turned to Anita and said, "Tell her everything is going well. I've got a few things left to do, and then I'll be done."

Anita and I agreed that she should indeed share this vision with Rhonda even though we were not sure what it meant or why she had received it. After all that Rhonda's family had endured over the last year, we hoped the vision would be helpful to them in some way.

When Anita and Rhonda were together two days

later, Anita shared what she had seen. Rhonda's eyes expanded as they welled up with tears.

She told Anita, "My parents loved the beach. It was their favorite place. When the kids all left home, my father took early retirement and they moved from New York to Florida. They both remarked often that those were the best, happiest times of their life together. I can't wait to tell Mom."

Rhonda's brain began to stir, and she explained to Anita that her grieving mother, Rose, had just taken her sister, Lisa, to visit Lourdes, the sacred shrine in France. They hoped to encounter the healing presence of God in the waters there. At Lourdes, Rose and Lisa had prayed for Lisa's cancer and for healing from it.

Rose had also asked God for a sign to let her know that James was fine. Rose's prayer life had been focused on James and the state of his soul for some time. She yearned to know whether he was in purgatory and how he was doing.

As Rhonda calculated what all this meant (her father's death, her sister's cancer, a vision, her mother and sister's trip to Lourdes), she asked Anita, "When did you have the dream?"

Anita replied, "On Saturday night. Why do you ask?"

Rhonda responded, "That was the day Mom and Lisa visited the water at Lourdes. My mother just received her sign."

Anita had not known about the trip to Lourdes, or of Rose's concerns for her deceased husband's soul and state. She had only received a vision in a dream, and had passed it on without having any idea what it might mean.

God had been at work in a way that can only be described as a marvelous mystery. Anita introduced us to the mystery of God in our own bedroom.

Mystics, Mysteries and Padre Pio too!

As Protestants, Anita and I did not have help with ways to understand the mysteries we encountered in her occasional dreams and visions. We knew they were from God, but we were careful not to discuss openly their content or meaning. Our experience in Protestant settings was that dreams and visions were usually received with puzzled looks and with skepticism, so we kept our experiences to ourselves.

However, as we were introduced to the Catholic Church, we met spiritual family members like Saints Teresa of Avila, Catherine of Siena and Padre Pio. Mystics were not pushed aside from the Church; they took up residence near the very heart of it.

We heard about places like Fatima and Lourdes, where the mystery of God abounds. Places we knew nothing about, but places that fascinated us because they seemed to jibe with our own divine encounters. This was new terrain for us. Even though Anita has not converted to Catholicism, the Church has been helpful to her in discerning the gift God has given her.

As we explored the Church, we discovered mystery residing at every turn. Of course, we begin each Mass by preparing to celebrate "these sacred mysteries." With incense, color, and the the body and blood of Christ, the Mass is filled with awe and wonder. In fact, John Paul II went so far as to describe the Mass as "heaven on earth... a mysterious participation in the heavenly liturgy."

The Catholic Church embraces mystery and even encourages it. How else do you explain the incorruption of the bodies of so many Catholic saints? Of course, all saints must have miracles attributed and documented to them in order to be canonized. That alone is mysterious enough. But, in addition to that, more than one hundred saints' bodies have remained almost entirely intact even decades and centuries after their deaths.

These saints' bodies were not treated or embalmed in most cases but rather were found incorruptible in form - lifelike, flexible, and even sweetly scented many years after death. Observers often found clear oils and fresh blood proceeding from these holy relics. This odd, mysterious and miraculous phenomenon of the incorruptibles has existed only since early Christian days, and Joan Carrol Cruz provides an excellent inspiring account of many of these claims in her work, *The Incorruptibles*.

St. Rita of Cascia's body is still fragrant some 500 years after her death. St. Teresa of Avila was found in a coffin nine months after her death. Although Teresa's clothing was made of dirty and rotten fabric fragments, her body was not only fresh and intact but it was mysteriously fragrant as well. Teresa's strange incorruptibility continued over many years and multiple exhumations.

But the most amazing example of this incorruptibility is that of Saint Andrew Bobola from the 17th century. A native of Poland, St. Andrew was captured by the Cossacks, received a cruel beating, and was dragged by horse through the countryside. He eventually was burned, half-strangled, partly flayed alive, and finally murdered by saber. Forty years after his death, St. Andrew's body was found incorrupt in a tomb under the ruins of a church in Pinsk, Poland. The condition of the body, which has never been embalmed, treated, or conditioned, has been declared a miraculous preservation in spite of its mutilated condition. It is still well preserved in a church in Warsaw. Andrew Bobola eventually was made a saint, and there have now been over 410 authenticated miracles attributed to him.

The Church understands that we will not always encounter God in predictable, transactional ways. God Himself is a great mystery and operates however He chooses.

The Church, for its part, helps to create a map for our divine encounters. By gathering all the experiences of those who have gone before us, we can generate something like a navigational map to help us understand how God is at work in the world and our lives. This is why tradition matters so much. We stand on the shoulders, and learn from the experiences, of those travelers who have gone before us. The Church gathers the dreams, visions, and mysteries of the saints to produce a map to assist the rest of us in our own journeys.

In Padre Pio's life and ministry, especially as

shared by Peggy Noonan (in *John Paul the Great*), we meet a man who defied normal human comprehension. Pope John Paul II agreed that Pio exhibited extraordinary spiritual gifts that could only be classified as a mystery.

Famous for his healing gifts and his ability to read souls, Padre Pio became noted for his confrontational style in the confessional. Were he to perceive that you were not disclosing the full truth about your actions, he would remind you of the facts. It was as if he knew your soul better than you did. Should you specifically deny the facts, Padre Pio would throw you out of the confessional altogether.

Padre Pio also evidenced the gift of appearing at two places simultaneously - the gift of "bi-location." Literally seen by witnesses with him in different places at the exact same moment, Pio's unique gifts became so commonplace that an assistant, when asked about Pio's whereabouts, would merely respond, "He's on bilocation."

According to tradition, a young Polish priest, Karol, came to see Padre Pio in 1947. Karol went to the confessional and knelt. As he did so, Pio rose from his chair, and knelt, saying that Karol would one day be a great pope. Only two people were there, and both are now dead. Neither Pope John Paul II nor Padre Pio ever spoke of that moment again.

However, John Paul II did reveal that a miracle came as a result of the meeting. John Paul II had worked with a close friend, Dr. Wanda Poltawska, on a book about sexual ethics and marriage. The Pope had known her for years, ever since she was arrested by the Nazis and freed five years later from a concentration camp. In 1962, Dr. Poltawska was stricken with terminal cancer. When she was scheduled for surgery, Cardinal Wojtyla at the time wrote Padre Pio and asked him to pray for Dr. Poltawska.

When she went for her pre-operative X-rays, the cancer had disappeared completely. Five years later, in 1967, Dr. Poltawska went to San Giovanni Rotondo to attend morning Mass. She hoped to meet Padre Pio in person in order to thank him for his intercessory prayers. Although she hoped to thank him personally, the big crowd swelled so greatly that there simply was no way for her to get anywhere near Pio.

As Mass ended, Padre Pio walked by Dr. Poltawska and stopped. He looked into her eyes and spoke. "Now are you all right?"

Padre Pio and Dr. Poltawska had never before met in person. At this moment, however, he knew exactly who she was, and he remembered having prayed specifically for her.

Padre Pio was made a saint in 2002.

Paul, Pio, Visions and Blood

For fifty years, Padre Pio bore the wounds of Jesus on his own hands, feet, and side. He manifested physically the stigmata, the marks of Christ. Deep bleeding wounds in the same places where Jesus had been nailed or wounded on the cross.

Jesus suffered from five separate wounds at His crucifixion. The wounds caused by a crown of thorns;

the scourging on His back; the wound in the side, caused by a spear; nail holes in His wrists, or hands; and nail holes in His ankles, or feet.

To help us understand this wonderful mystery, in Galatians 6:17, Paul writes words that can only be characterized as "mysterious."

*Finally, let no one cause me trouble, for **I bear on my body the marks of Jesus.***

What exactly does the Apostle Paul mean with these words about bearing the "marks of Jesus"? This is the only place in the Bible where the stigmata (the Greek word translated as the "marks" of Jesus) are mentioned. Paul uses the same verb "to bear" as the word used to describe how Jesus "bore" the cross, so he is linking his own wounds to those of Jesus at the cross.

Here is Paul writing that he bears the wounds of Jesus on his own body. Believers have wondered for millennia exactly what this means, but as a Protestant, I never once heard mention of this verse, or of the stigmata, by anyone ever. We completely ignored the subject.

St. Paul may be revealing that he bore the stigmata, the wounds of Jesus. If this is the case, bruises and bleeding made themselves real in his palms or on other places of Paul's body. Since the time of Paul, more than 500 persons have exhibited such stigmata. Saints Catherine, Francis, and Pio all manifested these same wounds each in their own unique ways.

How could this be? It is a holy mystery.

On October 22, 1918, Padre Pio wrote to his spiritual advisor, Padre Benedetto, describing how he received the stigmata.

On the morning of the 20th of last month, in the choir, after I had celebrated Mass, I yielded to a drowsiness similar to a sweet sleep. **All the internal and external senses and even the very faculties of my soul were immersed in indescribable stillness.** *Absolute silence surrounded and invaded me. I was suddenly filled with great peace and abandonment which effaced everything else and caused a lull in the turmoil. All this happened in a flash.*

While this was taking place, **I saw before me a mysterious person similar to the one I had seen on the evening of 5 August. The only difference was that his hands and feet and side were dripping blood.** *The sight terrified me and what I felt at that moment is indescribable. I thought I should die and really should have died if the Lord had not intervened and strengthened my heart which was about to burst out of my chest.*

The vision disappeared and I became aware that my hands, feet and side were dripping blood. *Imagine the agony I experienced and continue to experience almost every day.* **The heart wound bleeds continually, especially from Thursday evening until Saturday.**

Dear Father, I am dying of pain because of the wounds and the resulting embarrassment I feel in my soul. **I am afraid I shall bleed to death if the Lord does not hear my heartfelt supplication to relieve me of this condition.** *Will Jesus, who is so good, grant me this grace? Will he at least free me from the embarrassment*

*caused by these outward signs? I will raise my voice and will not stop imploring him until in his mercy he takes away, not the wound or the pain, which is impossible since I wish to be inebriated with pain, but **these outward signs which cause me such embarrassment and unbearable humiliation.***
(Letters 1, No. 511)

St. Francis is the first recorded believer to exhibit such wounds when he did so in the 13th century. St. Catherine of Siena then manifested the stigmata in the 14th century, and St. Teresa of Avila is even reported to have died in the 16th century with a stigmatic heart that revealed the piercing of a spear. In other words, Padre Pio experienced in the 20th century the same bleeding wounds that stigmatics have shared for centuries.

Stigmatic Surgery

The stigmata never even entered my mind until my own surgery in June 1993. Remember with me a few of the details leading up to the removal of my colon and its replacement with a plastic bag on my midriff.

Our family had moved to Yale for me to pursue the Ph. D. Degree in New Testament and Ancient Christian Origins. My wife and I had been married three years at the time. We had two small children, and we were a thousand miles away from our nearest family members. I was growing desperately ill with colitis, which introduced me to pain in a new way each day. My academic performance was sub-par.

We felt isolated and unprepared for the challenges. Until this point, both of us had lived fairly comfortable lives. For the first time in our lives, we were experiencing a real test.

The only good news was the extra energy added from steroid usage to combat my colitis propelled me to complete the degree in record time. I became the first person in over thirty years at Yale to complete the degree in three years, the first since my own professor had done it. Other than that one achievement, life was miserable.

Our fears as a couple increased. Why have we moved to New England? To suffer like this? What is the point? We have tried to be faithful, and this is what we get?

Our prayers became more plaintive: "We are trying to be obedient here, Lord. Where in the world are you?"

Just like we had experienced with the visions and dreams of Anita, our Protestant experience had no means to explain the suffering we were enduring. Like Job, we encountered various people who told us their own theories of suffering:

1. You must be disobeying God and be doing something outside of God's will. Stop and your suffering will end. This is God's way of correcting you.

   or

2. We have no idea what is going on. Just pray and let's hope God does something to help

you and your family.

Obviously, no one can fully explain suffering or its meaning. However, in this time, through the Catholic Church, I discovered mystics like John of the Cross and Teresa of Avila who did not recoil or blanch in the face of suffering. Rather, they saw suffering as an opportunity to meet God. They taught me that suffering often draws us closer to God. Instead of being a sign of God's punishment or distance, suffering can purify us, lead us into the heart of God, and transform our souls.

After two years of suffering without a cure, I agreed to the surgery to have my entire colon removed. I would not be 100%, but I would be close. As my surgeon put it, "It's a radical cure, but it's a cure."

After surgery, I awoke in the hospital with tubes coming out of every orifice on my body plus a few new ones the surgeon had created. My body was trying to wean itself off the high dosage of steroids to which I had become accustomed.

I lay on my back, staring at my mid-section where I had a large wound with staples holding my body together. The incision went from just beneath my sternum down to my pelvis. The staples formed what almost appeared like a cross on my body. The wound ached and prevented me from moving without much pain and discomfort.

I lay in that bed for three days. Because my wife was suffering a miscarriage in the very same week, my primary visitor was my friend, Father Steven.

He would come and sit in the chair next to my bed. Usually, he would say nothing unless I spoke first. His presence alone communicated immense grace and love. He was there, and that was all I needed to know.

One afternoon, as Father Steven stood to leave, I asked him to pray with me. As we prayed, the presence of God enveloped my body. An intense light filled my eyes, warmth surrounded me, and my body ceased feeling or movement. I became speechless as I stared at the wound on my torso, overcome in awe with the presence of God.

As Father Steven finished praying, I said, "Something just happened. It was almost like a vision. My wound became a cross. It sounds bizarre, but it reminded me of Galatians 6:17 and the marks of Christ."

He thought for a moment. "The nuns I introduced you to spend their days hoping to have just one experience like this in their lives. This is a special experience you just had, and it may take you years to understand it completely."

The pain did not go away. The wound was not healed. In fact, the wound still presents challenges today, and I occasionally receive reminders of the pain in my body when I am unable to do some of the things I could do before my colon was removed.

But something deep and rich had taken place on that hospital bed. In my suffering, for a minute, maybe two, I had been transformed in a new way. God had held me closer than I had ever known. For a moment, I had merged into His grace. He had touched my eyes, enabling me to see my wound and my suffering in a new way.

My suffering had not been a sign of God's absence after all; rather, He had used my suffering to do something new in me. Not only shaping my spirit to have more compassion for those who are suffering, God also drew me close and changed me from the inside out. He drew me into Himself, to His very heart.

Suffering can lead to transformation. And redemption. A marvelous mystery.

God reveals Himself through human reason and intelligence to be sure. But even more, God's glory is shrouded in mystery.

That mystery lies hidden in the walls of this old house. I discovered it in the bedroom. In fact, this house provides maps to understand God's mystery whenever you meet Him.

"Everything you need is in this house."

FAMILY CEMETERY

Chickens in the yard, abortion cemetery near the parking lot,
and an elderly priest wearing high-tops.

Cemeteries make good neighbors.
In fact, after Anita and I got married, a cemetery was our very first neighbor. It was wonderful. After all, cemeteries are quiet. Then again, come to think of it, cemeteries can speak very loudly when they need to.

Lessons from a Cemetery with Chickens

My seminary training required me to attend worship in a faith or tradition different from my own. Since we lived in a small Georgia town, with no Jewish, Muslim, or Hindu places of worship, I chose to sample a Catholic Mass. Nestled on a beautiful tract of land donated to the church by the famous actress, Susan Hayward, and her husband, Our Lady of Perpetual Help Church became my destination. I learned later that Hayward and her husband were both adult converts to the Church. Knowing that ahead of time might have served as a good warning to me!

My car rounded the curve on a lovely country road. As I turned into the driveway of the small, rural congregation, nothing could have prepared me for the jarring sight on my left.

At the edge of the parking lot, hundreds of small white crosses lined the hillside. In fact, they populated the hill. At the top of the hill stood a an enormous single large cross. At the base of the hill, beneath the rows of crosses, a sign read, "In Memory of the Millions of Children's Lives Ended by Abortion."

Nothing prepared me for my arrival into that parking lot at Our Lady of Perpetual Help. The abortion memorial cemetery literally took my breath away, and I have ever since referred to that place as the family cemetery.

In my mainline Protestant existence as a Methodist and in my coursework at seminary, we rarely talked about abortion. It was viewed as just another touchy topic where people held lots of strong opinions.

When I meet most Catholic priests, I marvel at how well-trained they are in theology, history, and philosophy. How they have such a strong foundation from which to make moral statements on various issues in life, like abortion in our culture. While I know a number of very pure, very motivated, very effective Protestant pastors, I have to admit I am amazed at the paucity of my training to be a Methodist pastor. We received almost no training whatsoever in areas as rudimentary as philosophy or moral thought.

So that hillside cemetery jarred my eyes and my spirit. It stopped me in my tracks and made me pause. What *did* I believe about abortion? Is it acceptable to end the lives of innocent unborn children for any reason?

The Methodist Church, in typical mainline Protestant fashion, avoided taking a bold, clear stance on abortion (and on most social issues for that matter). Every four years, representatives of the Methodist Church would vote on the official position regarding abortion. Rather than staking out a clear position, based on Scripture, moral principles and reasoning, the representatives would simply vote. With teaching formed in a political process, the Methodist Church worked hard not to hurt anyone's feelings. The goal was to be inclusive. My goal was truth.

Methodist positions, decisions, and a good portion of doctrinal thinking, are set by what is called the General Conference. This conference meets one time for two weeks every four years and possesses the ultimate word of authority on all things Methodist, including the official positions on abortion and life issues. This conference is comprised of 1000 persons, half lay, half clergy, who are popularly elected by regions throughout the country. Oddly, the bishops of the Methodist Church have no vote on matters before the conference itself. In other words, the elected leaders (yes, bishops are popularly elected too) do not participate in the decisions about doctrinal and social stances. They merely serve as regional administrators for what is decided at the General Conference.

In fact, the Methodist Church is set up very much like the federal government with its three branches: executive (bishops), legislative (General Conference), and judicial (Judicial Council). And its decisions are made by popularly elected delegates, many of whom have no theological or moral training whatsoever and a number of whom seldom or rarely attend their own churches. They simply navigate the Methodist political process well and then arrive to debate and pronounce on all things doctrinal and ecclesiastical.

It makes sense, then, that I was shocked by the sight of a small rural Catholic church in Carrollton, Georgia, who had the boldness to take a clear stance on the intrinsically evil act of terminating the lives of the pre-born. I knew that taking such a strong stance brings pushback and criticism.

Clear stances force persons to agree or disagree. Those who disagree often leave churches or with-hold donations. That pushback is why the Methodist church hemmed and hawed and even contradictorily provided funds at the same time both to groups who opposed and also groups who advocated abortion. That way, no one would get their feelings hurt.

The contrast hit me like a freight train in the middle of the night. Upon merely pulling into the parking lot, I encountered the Church who is not afraid to speak Truth, regardless of the public response or the pushback that comes with it. I had never even considered that that Church might exist.

This abortion memorial cemetery meant that the Church really and honestly stood for something. The Catholic Church's position was clear. Sadly, I was accustomed to every man for himself when it came to matters of doctrine and conscience.

The picture of that cemetery will remain in my head forever because the family cemetery made me reconsider what I thought about important questions like:

On whose authority does the Church stand?

By what authority does the Church proclaim Truth?

And does the Church trust that authority more than any poll of public opinion?

In that same parking lot, the cemetery lay on the left, but straight ahead of me sat a small house, the rectory, with chickens and dogs running around in the front yard. It was almost as if I had arrived at the abode of St. Francis of Assisi, simple and joyful.

As Mass began, Father Regan, a short, rotund, radiant man entered from the sacristy. Beneath his vestments, he was wearing Nike high-tops. Chickens in the yard, abortion cemetery near the parking lot, and an elderly priest wearing high-tops. My seminary assignment to experience a worship tradition entirely was already stretching me in new ways!

Feeling awkward and out of place in a Catholic church, I sat alone in the back corner of the church, taking a few notes for my assignment. With Mass underway, I looked around at the people in the half-full church for the Saturday vigil. Normal people were reciting words and performing rituals I knew nothing about. To my left, in the opposite back corner of the church, sat a man by himself, reading a newspaper. Not reading discreetly with the paper in his lap. No, this man held the newspaper high and scanned it page by page as the Mass proceeded. He seemed completely oblivious to the Mass transpiring around us.

I had already learned (Chapter 1) that the Catholic Church is mean when a woman stuck her finger in my chest to prohibit me from communion. This man in the back pew was teaching me that the Catholic Church is boring! Now I knew the Church was mean *and* boring.

I was completely out of my comfort zone. First, the family cemetery; then, the St. Francis-like rectory; and now, the utter disengagement of the man across the aisle from me. Suddenly, as Father Regan invited the congregation to the altar to receive the elements, the newspaper reader set down his paper and went forward to commune with God. When he returned, the man gathered his belongings and left the building.

This entire visit had taught me three new things about the Catholic Church.

1. The Catholic Church certainly stood for something. An abortion cemetery proved that.
2. The Catholic Church marched to a different drummer as evidenced by the odd priest and his home.
3. The Catholic Church was boring. Otherwise, how else do you explain a man sitting in the back of the church reading a newspaper until he could receive the elements? In my own tradition, being relevant and engaging ranked at the top of the priority list.

I had no idea what was going on here.

Paul's Lesson to Timothy on Authority

There where false teachers in the church in Ephesus. By writing 1st Timothy, Paul wants Timothy to remain in Ephesus to prevent the congregation from deviating from the Truth.

At the end of the first half of the letter, Paul zeroes in on the core of the matter at 1st Timothy 3:14-16. The core is the Truth of the faith.

> *I hope to come to you soon, but I am writing these instructions to you so that, if I am delayed, you may know how one ought to behave in the **household of God, which is the church of the living God, the pillar and bulwark of the truth**.*
> *Without any doubt, **the mystery of our religion is great:***
> *He was **revealed** in flesh,*
> ***vindicated** in spirit,*
> ***seen** by angels,*
> ***proclaimed** among Gentiles,*
> ***believed in** throughout the world,*
> ***taken up** in glory. (3:14-16)*

Without this core doctrine and Truth, the Church will wander into error, and that error will lead to other problems in leadership and worship because Truth establishes the foundation of the church.

In verse 15, Paul teaches them how to behave in the household of God which is the *church of the living God, the pillar and bulwark of the truth*. The church is the pillar and bulwark of the Truth, not the bellwether of public opinion or of the declarations of the pastor. Truth is not up for a vote. And Truth lives in the Church.

Immediately following his claim that the Church is the pillar of the Truth, St. Paul provides a six line hymn, which summarizes that Truth.

The Apostle Paul reaffirms here in a very direct way that the authority and the Truth reside in the Church. Not in the mind of each individual believer, nor in the results of a popular vote, nor in Scripture alone. But in the *Church*. The Church uses her tradition, her Scriptures, and her magisterium (teaching authority) to discern and share the Truth.

Once the Church loses the Truth, the Church becomes just another group of humans like a civic group, a country club or a neighborhood tennis team.

In order to ensure that he is clear, Paul reminds Timothy in this little six line hymn what comprises the Truth. Here is the Truth from 1st Timothy 3.

> *Jesus*
> *was revealed...,*
> *was vindicated...,*
> *was seen...,*
> *was proclaimed...,*
> *was believed...,*
> *was taken up...*
> *(3:15-16)*

Notice how the Truth centers on Jesus. *He* is the substance of our faith.

What's first? The incarnation. *Jesus was revealed*

in the flesh.

He was vindicated in the spirit. Jesus displayed the power of the Spirit of God and received the approval of the Spirit at His baptism and at other times.

He was seen by angels. Jesus existed with God before He became fully human. He was raised at His resurrection and celebrated by the angels at the tomb.

He was proclaimed among Gentiles, or among the nations. Jesus *is* the content of our faith. He is what we proclaim. Ours is not a set of ideas or moral teachings or rules to keep. We desire a relationship with Jesus. Everything else flows from Him.

He was believed in throughout the world. This is not *a* truth for some people, or some region. Jesus is *the* Truth for all people. Everywhere.

He was taken up in glory. Jesus returned to His place in and with God. He was not a mere man. He has conquered death, and His resurrection is real. We are Easter people.

Paul passes on the Truth of the faith in 1st Corinthians in the exact same way in 1st Corinthians 15. This is important because it shows how consistent the Church was, and continues to be, about the Truth.

*Now I should remind you, brothers and sisters, of the **good news that I proclaimed to you**,*
which you in turn received, in which also you stand,
through which also you are being saved, if you hold firmly to the message that I proclaimed to you—unless you have come to believe in vain.
For I handed on to you as of first importance what I in turn had received:

*that **Christ died** for our sins in accordance with the scriptures,*
*and that He was **buried**,*
*and that He was **raised** on the third day in accordance with the scriptures,*
*and that He **appeared** to Cephas, then to the twelve.*
***Then He appeared** to more than five hundred brothers and sisters at one time, most of whom are still alive, though some have died.*
***Then He appeared** to James, then to all the apostles.*
*Last of all, as to someone untimely born, **He appeared** also to me. (15:1-8)*

When Paul shares the core of the Truth, he says, "*This is what I received.*" Paul hands on what he has received. This is the *tradition of the Church*. Paul stands in the line of those who have received the Truth from the Church. Paul has no scripture to rely on because there was no New Testament in the first century. Paul is not even aware that he is writing a letter that will become sacred scripture in the years that follow.

Notice how Paul is not making up Truth or the content of the faith as he goes. Nor is he asking for the Corinthians' approval. Paul writes down the tradition he has received because Truth comes from the Church. Paul inherits and passes on doctrine as a part of the Church. He does the very same thing in 1st Timothy as he does here in 1st Corinthians. Consistent.

In 1st Corinthians, just like in 1st Timothy, the emphasis is on Jesus. He is the content of our faith because Jesus *is* the Truth. Consistent.

Paul's words of 1ˢᵗ Timothy 3:15, "*the church of the living God, the pillar and bulwark of the truth*," reveal where the Truth resides: in the Church, the pillar, the bulwark. And Jesus is that Truth.

Doctrine by Democracy

Since I was a leader in the evangelical movement of the United Methodist Church, I naturally played some role in leadership for the denomination. That leadership often occurred behind the scenes.

Every four years, the newly-elected 1000 delegates to the General Conference gather to vote on whether Methodists would consider abortion to be moral or immoral for the next four years. Abortion and life matters were therefore not so much issues of doctrine or truth to be discerned but rather of political influence to be exerted. Just like the American political arena.

In order to help the Methodist Church find and maintain a moral compass on issues regarding the dignity of human life, several colleagues and I would raise money every four years to work to ensure that some delegates would be elected to General Conference to represent an orthodox, historic Christian perspective. We hoped the Methodist Church would embrace that all humans, the born and the unborn, are created by God in the image of God.

It still surprises me that my already large responsibilities as a pastor were forced to expand to include two years of advance planning and fund-raising simply to hope delegates would vote on sound doctrine every fourth year. That meant I also realized that the truth, not Truth, would be decided every four years on the whim of a vote.

In retrospect, I realize how utterly absurd my mindset had become. We gather every four years to vote on whether abortion is going to be moral for the upcoming four years? And we base our vote on what authority? And the people voting may have no theological training at all and may not even be actively involved in spiritual formation and discipleship in their own churches? How did we arrive at such a way to govern and form a Church?

This weighed heavily on my conscience. How can you help lead a group that operates like a political party more than a people of Truth?

Who controls the moral compass from which you lead?

The Methodist Church, like nearly every Protestant group, also has almost no teaching on marriage, family, and children. That created lots of awkward situations, like meeting a couple planning to be married, when I had no official teaching with which to instruct them or to base the decision for marriage. In our time together, the couple might share that one had been married three times, the other twice. Because the Methodist Church has no teaching on marriage, every pastor would decide matters like this for himself or herself. As a pastor you knew that any wedding you would not perform would easily be blessed by another Protestant pastor down the street. Much like a judge whose ruling was overturned on appeal because the appeals are unlimited.

As our marriage grew and matured, Anita and I discovered, really by accident, that marriage really is a sacrament. This idea was absent from my training and background since Protestants view marriage simply as just one of the things the Church does.

Anita and I discovered that marriage is not merely a matter of convenience or something to be negotiated. Marriage is a divine covenant, not a mere contract between humans. In marriage, the spouses' physical intimacy becomes a sign and a pledge of spiritual communion. God is at work in a marriage in a remarkable way to join the two into one and to bless the lives of children and families. It is indissoluble.

I now served a significant church and led in a denomination that allowed each pastor to make it up as he went, while I viewed marriage as something entirely different.

This particular conflict happened often, and sometimes the results were not pretty. In my very first pastorate, a man in the congregation asked me to perform a wedding for a friend of his who wanted to marry his live-in girlfriend of the last eight years. When I expressed concern that I did not even know the couple, the man immediately began to pressure me, saying, "Would you prefer that they just live together instead of being married?" As if that were the only alternative.

As a Methodist pastor, I knew I had no backup on this subject. The decision was entirely up to me. The Methodist Church had no position on what marriage is or what the expectations were from the

Church. I could perform the wedding if I wanted to make this church member happy, or I could wrestle with whether performing the marriage really was a good thing. I could choose to lose the member and his family from a church that only had about 70 people on any given Sunday. Not a fun place to be for a young man just a few months into his first role as a pastor.

Later in my ministry, an elderly woman asked me, "How do you say with a straight face, 'Until death do you part?' when you perform the marriage of a couple already married multiple times?" I had no answer. Worse, I was embarrassed at my own hypocrisy. Marrying couples who had been in serial marriages felt like a charade. After all, the words were clear. *What God has joined together, let no man put asunder.* And *until death do you part.*

What *did* we mean by those words? I really had no idea. Were we merely asking God to bless something that we wanted rather than asking what God Himself wanted? And, again, my denomination had no position or teaching authority to back me up if my own understanding offended the couple at hand.

My own hypocrisy confronted me most painfully when I served on the board that voted on candidates seeking to be ordained as Methodist pastors. Because my views did not jibe with the general denomination, I grew accustomed to being on the losing end of votes regarding candidates.

We regularly evaluated candidates for ministry who had been married multiple times, candidates who had left their families in order to become pastors when their spouse was unsupportive, and candidates who said they did not agree with the denomination on many things but would support those teachings until they could help change them in an upcoming vote. On one occasion, we even voted to ordain a person who had been married five times.

These annual week-long meetings filled me with despair. Anita came to dread my attending them at all because she knew what I would be like when I returned home.

In each meeting, I stared our lack of clear teaching, the complete lack of doctrinal authority, and the absence of shared beliefs in the face, and it left me emotionally despondent. We really stood for nothing. We had nothing in common except our Methodist name and official logo. As a result, everyone just did as they pleased.

I knew I did not fit. I was reaching middle age, standing at the top of the Methodist heap, and I felt like a hypocrite. I supported a system that had no idea where it stood on life, abortion, marriage, and children. And I had no idea what to do about it. I knew very well what I believed, but it happened to coincide with what the Catholic Church taught. In practice, the Catholic Church had become my authority.

My spirit became divided, developing a kind of spiritual schizophrenia. In one part of my spiritual mind, I thoroughly loved being a pastor at such a wonderful church. The ministries of that place were and are extraordinary. The people are nothing short of remarkable. On the other hand, the lack of any doctrinal definition, or even clarity, eroded the foundation from beneath my feet. Worse, the system was set up to prevent any clarity or definition.

We were a people without a foundation, without any sense of tradition or Truth. Worst of all, not only would the truth be popularly decided every four years, it also would go unenforced in the work of the Church. We had no leader to ensure that bishops enforced the handful of positions or doctrines of the Methodist Church. It truly was every man and woman for himself. At best, it was doctrine by democracy; at worst, it was doctrinal anarchy.

Not to mention that, as a leader of a very large church, I was required to foot the bill for behaviors in the denomination which disgusted me, and I had no recourse. In fact, the supervisor assigned to oversee our region of congregations would often tell me I was on my own when it came to doctrine or belief. Just be sure to send in the money our congregation was expected to supply. In other words, "We are making it up as we go. And please keep the checks coming."

Here I was a leader in a denomination seeking tolerance and inclusiveness more than it sought the Truth my heart yearned for. Inclusiveness may be a small part of the Truth, but it is not Truth itself. It is a cheap, shallow substitute that the world has created in its own image.

An organizational and leadership nightmare. Bishops and pastors with responsibility but no authority. An institution with no head or leader.

In the moments when my hypocrisy felt greatest,

I came to remember the family cemetery, that little abortion memorial of crosses. There was a Church who knew where it stood. While I felt like a hypocrite, here was a Church who, albeit imperfectly, sought to put its money where its mouth was.

Here was a Church who was intent on recognizing that intrinsically evil acts are just that: intrinsically evil.

Here was a Church who loved marriage and sought to lift it to its highest peak not settle for whatever any person wanted.

Here was a Church who believed some things really are not matters of opinion. Some things are wrong whether we like it or not.

And here was a Church who stood tall in the culture and said, "No," to the absurd ideas of political correctness and the tolerance of evil.

And that Church also had Little Agnes, a tiny woman who spoke volumes to me about the Truth foundation on which believers stand.

Little Agnes

Agnes grew up comfortable in a loving family. At the age of 18, she heard God calling. "Serve me."

In loving response to God, Agnes became a teacher in a Christian school in perhaps the poorest city in the world where she taught for twenty years.

When she walked down the street and came upon a woman dying in the gutter in front of the hospital, God moved in a new way and invited her to move to serve firsthand the desperately poor living in the trenches, slums, and gutters. From that moment, she knew her life was for the poorest of the poor.

Agnes invested 24 hours a day with lepers, the poor, the sick, abandoned children, and hungry wanderers on the streets and in the slums. Agnes gave herself over completely to the Lord.

She loved Jesus and desired nothing more than to be united with Him in her service. Other women began popping up at her doorstep asking if they too could help serve the vulnerable and desperate. Eventually, hundreds of women arrived to help Agnes care for the people everyone else had forgotten.

Physically tiny, Agnes possessed a strong spirit. Like the Apostle Paul before her, she was willing to suffer in order to serve and that made her a leader. Not her training. Not her powers of public speaking. Nor her family lineage.

No, Agnes stood on the authority of the Church and poured herself out in the slums and gutters, and beside the death beds. Others saw greatness in her selfless servant leadership. And they arrived to follow her lead.

When someone really embraces the truth that the more you give your life to God, the more you will have, soon other people will follow. Deep inside, most of us are yearning to give ourselves over completely to God because this is what we were made for.

Fifty years after she met that first dying woman in the gutter, more than 3000 women in 517 missions (hospitals, homes, hospices) in 100 countries served alongside Agnes. She never recruited a single one.

This is how she became Mother Teresa of Calcutta.

Given her spiritual strength, it should not have come as a surprise when Teresa spoke so poignantly in 1994 at the National Prayer Breakfast in Washington. At the time she spoke, she was an internationally known servant leader, who passed on what she had received from the Church and then lived it out more powerfully than anyone else on earth.

When she spoke, the image was striking. This was not her opinion, one opinion among many. Here was a tiny little woman, standing on the Truth of the Church. This was the Truth she selflessly lived out decade after decade in the slums of Calcutta.

Imagine how President and Mrs. Clinton must have felt when they heard Mother Teresa say to the thousands of attendees:

> *And if we accept that a mother can kill even her own child, how can we tell other people not to kill one another? How do we persuade a woman not to have an abortion? As always, we must persuade her with love and we remind ourselves that love means to be willing to give until it hurts. Jesus gave even His life to love us. So, the mother who is thinking of abortion, should be helped to love... the father is told that he does not have to take any responsibility at all for the child he has brought into the world. The father is likely to put other women into the same trouble. So abortion just leads to more abortion. Any country that accepts abortion is not teaching its people to love, but to use any violence to get what they want. This is why the greatest destroyer of love and peace is abortion.*

Little Mother Teresa rebuked our entire Western culture of death. She rebuked our selfishness and our love of convenience. And she shamed us for our lack of love.

She stood on Truth mapped out by centuries of the Church's moral teaching and tradition. Her own life proved the validity of the Truth coming from her lips.

God's Exit Strategy

Serving as a Methodist pastor for nearly twenty years blessed my life and my family's life in many ways. We shared in the lives of people in ways I could never have imagined. We witnessed the transformation of persons and families. We formed friendships and bonds around the world with partners on every continent of the globe. The hungry were fed. The naked were clothed. Christ was shared.

In my final eight years as a pastor, I benefited tremendously from the leadership of one bishop, whose grace abounded to me, even when I confessed to him my struggles with life in the Methodist Church. Along the way, I shared a vision with that bishop of a mainstream talk radio program designed to engage people from every part of American culture.

When we launched that talk radio show as an extension of our church's ministries, we envisioned it as being a vehicle to communicate the love of God in a non-traditional way. The program discusses real life, in addition to politics and culture, from a distinctively faith-centered point of view. We focus on a moral compass, not on what's right or left but on what's right or wrong. Mainstream radio listeners discover in the Allen Hunt Show how faith plays a role in parenting, in workplaces, in politics, in sports, and in life.

We never envisioned that it would eventually become a daily, nationally syndicated show. My Methodist bishop, Lindsey Davis, was very supportive of what he saw as a creative way for the Church to interact with the culture in real, honest, open conversation. I am very grateful for his trust and support.

Ironically, as the show grew, my path veered in a way I had not anticipated. My preparations for on-air conversations about parenting, sexuality, and war all led me to the Catholic Church and its rich body of teaching and thought. The Church had invested centuries of thought in setting forth teaching and interpreting Scripture. In contrast, as a Protestant, I was on my own. My own Methodist tradition, and Protestantism in general, possessed very little clear thought when compared to the centuries of orthodox teaching and reflection of the Church.

As a Methodist, I had a lot of wallpaper but no house.

It surprised me that I often found myself speaking and thinking in a very Catholic way on the radio. Catholic clergy and laypersons frequently emailed to comment on how very Catholic I sounded for a Methodist preacher. They were right, but I could not see what they saw.

My own Catholicism was obvious to almost everyone except me.

Since I had learned to trust the Catholic Church on matters and issues for the show, I eventually discovered I could also trust the Catholic Church on issues where I had little preparation. Doctrines that often confound Protestants, like those revolving around Mary, purgatory, and the Pope, did not bother me. I had already learned to trust the Church.

Without even realizing it, I had snuck in the back door of the Church's teaching and discovered it to be solid and true. I had serendipitously discovered that the Church really is the pillar and bulwark of the Truth.

I delighted in having a Pope who stood for the Truth. It was a welcome change from the leadership vacuum of Methodism.

I became deeply grateful that a successor to Peter hands on what he has received just as the Apostle Paul had done in 1st Corinthians and in 1st Timothy. The Pope inspired me with his authority to ground the Church in Truth and not suffer from a continuous need to seek election or to take polls to ensure that the culture considers him or the Church "relevant."

Best of all, I appreciated how the Pope, through tradition, Scripture, and the magisterium, discerns and settles Truth for the Church. Most Protestants continually invoke Scripture as the sole source of authority for the Church, but it is obvious that Scripture must not be entirely clear. Otherwise, why would there be 33,000 varieties of Protestant Christianity all claiming to be based solely on Scripture?

If Scripture is so clear, why do Protestants agree on so little?

Moreover, if Scripture is the sole source of authority, why does it never claim that exclusive authority for itself?

Scripture is helpful, enlightening, and authoritative to be sure. Scripture is the Church's book. I love Scripture so much that I have devoted most of my adult life to studying and proclaiming its beauty. But at the same time, Scripture never claims sole authority for itself. Instead, Scripture points to the Church as the pillar and bulwark of the Truth. Who decided to place all authority in Scripture? Not the Church.

Most importantly, the Church birthed Scripture, not vice-versa.

The Church existed for centuries before the New Testament became the Church's measuring stick. The Church wrote, gathered, collected, and put together the books that became Scripture. Scripture belongs to the Church. It is not the other way around.

Truth lives in the Church, and Scripture helps reveal and define it. The *Church* is the pillar and bulwark, not Scripture. Remember the words of 1 Tim. 3:14 - ...*the household of God, which is the **church** of the living God, the pillar and bulwark of the truth.*

God arranged these pieces together for me in a wonderful mosaic. And as our show grew nationally, and eventually became a daily show, my mind cleared and clarity arrived on important issues.

I discovered how incredibly frustrating and discouraging it is to non-Christians to try to make sense of the 33,000 different Christian voices all claiming authority and all claiming emphases on particular matters. A non-believer usually wants a cup of water to drink, not an overwhelming fire hydrant of information regarding how one little group of believers is different and so much more right than some other little group of believers. All the division and fractiousness of Protestantism came to weigh heavily on my soul. That division sends a terrible message to the world.

Jesus prayed that we would be One. And He meant it.

After all, Jesus birthed just one Church.

It also became obvious that I could not pastor a mega-church and lead a daily radio show with all its demands. I needed to make a choice, so I spent several days in prayer by myself in the mountains. Trying to combat my own spiritual schizophrenia, and my own feelings of hypocrisy. Finally I confronted the questions that had percolated in my soul for more than a decade.

After much prayer, the choice became clear. God was calling me to serve as a missionary in American culture through a non-traditional radio show. I had lots of questions about how this might unfold, but the answer always came back in prayer, "Have the faith you teach others to have. Trust in Me."

Just as God was calling me to a new mission role, I was clearly becoming increasingly Catholic. For years, I had been wrestling within. Now I could no longer live with myself if I merely continued as is because it was the easy thing to do.

My sense of hypocrisy regarding issues of life and

marriage had been with me for some time. But in my final months as a Methodist pastor, I grew increasingly uncomfortable with my role in leading the celebration of communion. This had not been a problem for me up until now. That is when I knew.

When I led communion, deep within me, I knew I no longer believed as Methodists do that Jesus was just "especially present" in a spiritual way. Deep down, I knew. The last piece had come together. Communion embodied the real presence of Jesus Christ, and I did not need to continue leading people in communion. It was time to go home to the Catholic Church.

The early seed planted by Sister Rose regarding the real presence of Christ in the Eucharist was now coming to full bloom. That issue had always been the one area that caused me to resist becoming Catholic. I just could not get my head around that belief. But now it was clear.

With my spirit both burdened and exhilarated, I met first with my Methodist bishop to share with him my call to transition from my role as a pastor to a new role in talk radio. We mapped out a plan to ensure that my successor in the Methodist congregation would have every opportunity to succeed with my help. We sketched out how to communicate my transition from my role as pastor in a church who had loved me and my family generously for eight years.

Given that our congregation had undergone some very large expansions in mission and our physical plant, and because leading a mega-church is very different from other sized congregations, I offered to stay for up to several years to help pass the baton slowly to equip my successor with the shift in leadership needed to lead such a complex church. My bishop indicated that he did not think that plan would work. I then offered to stay for up to a year after my successor was in place to help him begin his new role and also to lead a capital campaign to fund the church's financial obligations. I also offered to receive no pay for that time so as not to be any burden on the congregation.

My heart's desire was to transition well and to fulfill the sacred trust that God and the bishop had given me in leading that great congregation. I wanted to cause as little disruption as possible.

In the end, I stayed for six months after my official finish date as Senior Pastor. The bishop asked the congregation to pay me a token stipend since I would be working for them in addition to my separate radio mission venture, which was funded entirely by donors who believed in its outreach. In that six months, we successfully completed the most generous capital campaign in the congregation's history. And I worked diligently to coach and offer wisdom to my successor to help him begin his ministry in that congregation so that he could stand on his own.

At the end of that six months, my role was no longer needed. I then moved forward with my personal decision to become fully Catholic. In a final meeting with my Methodist bishop, he showed tremendous grace and understanding. He thanked me for my leadership throughout the years and also for my hard work to transition my former congregation to a new leader. Even though he asked me to remain Methodist if I possibly could, he gave me his blessing when I shared that I no longer could do so with integrity.

God had revealed the treasures of the Church to me. Treasures hidden in the walls of the Church. Treasures available to every Catholic. Treasures like the Eucharist in the dining room, and the saints in the basement.

My journey had now arrived at its obvious destiny.

I threw myself at the mercy of the Church to become a Catholic in full communion, and the Church welcomed me with grace and hospitality.

Best of all, I welcomed the authority of the Church in my life. I no longer had to become the expert on every single issue of the Christian life so that I could stand alone and defend any position without backup. Mother Church, and her vast resources and centuries of thought and reflection, were now my own. Alongside tiny Mother Teresa, I could stand on the authority and teaching of the Church.

"Everything you need is in this house."

The family cemetery - that little abortion memorial - spoke volumes to the authority of the Church of the living God, the pillar and bulwark of the truth. A little gathering of crosses spoke a message of life to a culture of death.

At last, now I was a part of the Church.

That left just one treasure yet to experience.

FRONT PORCH

...this is the front porch of the entire world.

Want to know how to live longer and healthier? Have a front porch.

Believe it or not, the healthiest communities feature homes with front porches.

Porches cultivate and sustain a sense of community. Porches create social glue, and build strong neighborhoods. Porches help neighbors get to know each other. And that sense of belonging and community lengthens and enriches the residents' lives.

Here is a secret: we were made for each other. Front porches prove it.

Jesus Loves Front Porches

She said the strangest thing. On the very first day of class, my history professor uttered very provocative words. Among all the things I heard in that first semester of my seminary training in preparation to become a Methodist pastor, her comment still stands out most of all.

She would teach us the history of early Christianity - from the disciples in the book of Acts all the way through the first ten centuries of believers. To introduce herself to a nervous group of newcomers (us on that very first day), she shared some of her own interests and personal background. We learned that she was married, and we learned about her study in the area of St. Anthony and the first monastic communities.

Then she shared her passion.

Her passion? The driving motivation for her entire ministry centered on - the unity of the Church.

I still remember it. She said, "I believe that, when Jesus prayed for His followers to be perfectly one in His final prayer in John 17, He really and truly meant it."

Jesus desires for His followers to be one. I thought to myself, what *does* that look like?

I found it more than surprising that a professor in one of the thousands of Protestant groups should be concerned with trying to bring all the other, fractious thousands of Protestant groups together as one. How could that even be possible? And what topics would the various Protestant groups even acknowledge they had in common?

Each Protestant group usually focuses on its own particular unique reason for being and rarely offers common ground with any other group. Protestants tend to dwell on areas where they differ and seldom focus on what they have in common. Every group wants to feel special and believe they have it right.

So when the professor said that, it surprised me that a member of a Protestant group would spend concerted energy working to unite all the different splinters back into the one tree from which they came. There seemed to be no remote chance of success. It was absurd.

When the whole model is built on conflict and division, how do you reverse that and seek unity?

But her comments on the very first day of my pastoral training raised two questions.

What actually unifies us believers anyway?

What do all these Protestant groups really have in common in the first place?

I found the answer on the front porch of this old house.

Perfectly One

When Jesus completes His final instructions for His twelve disciples, He prays over them. No surprise there.

These disciples have learned from Jesus, served with Jesus, and lived with Him. These twelve men will become the foundation of a movement that shakes history and creates the most enduring global impact of all time. These men will launch the Church, the family of God. Imperfect men, chosen by Jesus, will reshape the world.

In His final words to them, Jesus reminds His twelve chosen men that believers will be known for their love. "Love one another."

Jesus then prays in order to prepare them for His

death. A prayer asking the Father to care for the twelve and the work they are about to lead. A prayer for all of His followers yet to come, including you and me. A prayer to bind us all together as one.

> *I ask not only on behalf of these, but also on behalf of those who will believe in me through their word, **that they may all be one**. As you, Father, are in me and I am in you, may they also be in us, so that the world may believe that you have sent me. The glory that you have given me I have given them, **so that they may be one, as we are one**, I in them and you in me, **that they may become perfectly one**, so that the world may know that you have sent me and have loved them even as you have loved me.*
> *(17:20–23*)*

Jesus' last message and prayer for His leaders consists of a prayer for unity. Jesus desires and prays for unity.

He expressly desires that we be *"perfectly* one."

In this prayer, Jesus three times prays for His followers to be one. Oneness is important to Jesus. It is a priority.

Jesus also desires for them to be one not just for their benefit but also for the sake of everyone else who will hear the Gospel through them. Their unity will impact the world.

How much more effective they will be if they stand as one against all that opposes the Church. Non-believers and newcomers will see that unity and be amazed that a group of people possesses such a powerful spiritual bond. It will stand in contrast to all the divisions and discord that fill the world.

Jesus says their unity reflects the unity of God Himself. Just as Jesus, the Father, and the Holy Spirit are one, so too, He says, should be those who are "in us."

The Trinity is one, and so too shall the body of the Church be. God, not our own efforts, is the source of our unity. Our oneness reflects the Oneness of God.

Finally, Jesus gives His "glory" to His followers in order to make them one. The glory of Jesus fuels and binds our unity. We do not merely decide to become unified on our own. The glory of God Himself is the binding agent. We taste that in the Eucharist.

Wow. These words need to be noted. Jesus means business.

These are not throwaway words. Jesus' desire is for us to be one as He and the Father, the Trinity, are One. *The unity of God is the model for the unity of the Church.*

We represent the unity of God in the world.

Jesus envisions a high destiny for His people: that they may become perfectly one. Not just one, but *perfectly* one. Completely unified. Not separated or divided in any way.

How in the world do you reconcile Jesus' strong and clear prayer with the 33,000 different ways we Christians have found to disagree?

Maybe, just maybe, division pleases us and not God. Perhaps discord is of our own sinful origin. Maybe, just maybe, the Church is designed to be built on the model of unity and not the model of division. Perhaps the unity of God should be our base rather than our tendency to accept conflict and division as normal.

Perfectly one. A beautiful and wonderful image.

When John Paul II first went back to Poland as the Pope in 1979, he celebrated Mass for a million people gathered in an open field. That single moment gave a picture of one Church, not separated into thousands of little divided groups, each with their own beliefs. Rather, one large mass of believers who formed a single spiritual family.

A million believers gathered *en* masse for *the* Mass. In a field, around the one altar, as if they were glued together by the Eucharist. The Eucharist and the real presence of Jesus bind us together. Remove that binding agent and you merely have a pile of bricks rather than a solid wall.

The Beautiful One

Thanksgiving. The Apostle Paul begins each of his letters to his churches in the same way, with a thanksgiving prayer. In first century style, his signature comes before the address name of the believers he is writing. Next, before launching into the body of the letter, Paul offers a thanksgiving prayer. He births each letter in prayer and gratitude to God.

Each thanksgiving prayer also provides a foretaste of what is coming in the rest of the letter. When we examined 1st Thessalonians earlier, we discovered what a warm, pastoral, affectionate letter Paul wrote. So it makes sense that he begins the letter with a simple, warm, affectionate prayer of thanksgiving in

1ˢᵗ Thessalonians 1:2.

> *We always **give thanks** to God for all of you and mention you in our prayers, constantly…*

To understand oneness, however, we need to look at Paul's letter to the Galatians. This letter is anything but warm and affectionate. Paul is as mad as a boiled owl. He is so furious that his anger with the divided, bickering Galatians shows up from the very beginning.

In contrast to all of his other letters, Paul begins Galatians with *no* thanksgiving at all.

> ***Paul an apostle—sent neither by human commission nor from human authorities, but through Jesus Christ and God the Father**, who raised Him from the dead— and all the members of God's family who are with me,*
>
> *To the churches of Galatia:*
>
> *Grace to you and peace from God our Father and the Lord Jesus Christ, who gave Himself for our sins to set us free from the present evil age, according to the will of our God and Father, to whom be the glory for ever and ever. Amen.*
>
> ***I am astonished that you are so quickly deserting the one** who called you in the grace of Christ and are turning to a different gospel— (Gal.1:1-6)*

Every part of the beginning of this letter differs from Paul's other letters. His signature reminds the Galatians that Paul is not deriving his authority from any human group but from God Himself. He immediately stakes out his authority against anyone who would teach in a way contrary to his own leadership.

Then notice the thanksgiving, right there between verse 5 and verse 6. It doesn't exist!

There is no thanksgiving at all. Paul is so livid at the Galatians that he cannot even bring himself to give thanks for them. He has no patience for people who have disappointed him so deeply. Instead, Paul is coming in to correct them.

Paul is astonished that they are abandoning the Gospel. Rather than trusting the grace of God in Jesus, many of the Galatians are retreating to Judaism, and obedience to the Old Testament Law and all the dietary and lifestyle rules that come with it.

In the past, they accepted the Gospel that St. Paul has planted in this church himself. Now, they have abandoned the teaching of the grace and love of Jesus Christ to embrace a different path altogether. Not so different from many of us still today who abandon a full life rooted in the abundant love of God in order to settle for a heavy life of mere rule-keeping.

The Apostle Paul spends the entire letter trying to remind them of who they are. His point: you are not Jewish Christians or Gentile Christians, you are Christians. You are "in Christ." Period. There is no other category.

Paul breaks down all those barriers, all those divisions, and all those man-made additions that we put onto the faith. Too often we work very hard to tear the Church apart into splinters. Instead Paul wants them to understand the simple truth: you are one in Christ.

This emphasis on oneness becomes most obvious in the centerpiece of the letter. The entire letter revolves around Galatians 3:26-28.

> *for* **in Christ Jesus you are all children of God through faith**. *As many of you as were baptized into Christ have clothed yourselves with Christ. There is no longer Jew or Greek, there is no longer slave or free, there is no longer male and female; for* **all of you are one in Christ Jesus**.

Paul's goal is simple and huge at the same time: to help them grasp the fact that they are one in Christ. Christ unifies, and Christ is enough. They need nothing else. Division is not of Him.

You have been baptized, *you* have been put into Christ, *you* are Gentiles and now *you* have been melded into *one* through your baptism in Christ Jesus. Jesus unifies all the people of God in Himself and His baptism.

To unify these bickering, divided people, Paul reminds them of the defining moment of baptism. Baptism is not just an initiation into the Church nor is it just a ceremony or a turning point. Baptism is the defining moment of divine transformation. Baptism is the common starting point for all believers. There are not different baptisms for different peoples. There is just one baptism because baptism flows from God through His Church.

In baptism, you leave that which is behind and are made a part of a new divine people. You become a part of the colony of heaven and a citizen of heaven. An eternally defining moment.

These verses are intended to perform an act, to *move* the people into unity. These words still perform that act on us. Baptism binds us together as the family of God.

Early Christians would disrobe when preparing to be baptized. Stepping into a pool of water, they would be baptized nude. After being baptized in the name of the Father, the Son, and the Holy Spirit, the newly baptized follower would emerge from the other side of the pool and receive a new white robe. This act represented the stripping off of your old, worldly way of life and being clothed in a new divine way of living.

In baptism, you are being washed and cleansed. You are being birthed by the Spirit. You put on a new white robe because you are a new creation. You now belong to God.

This divine transformation unifies us in the one Lord and Savior as a part of His One Universal Church. Division has no place.

We are one. May God forgive us when we splinter and divide over our own desires to be right or to be autonomous or to reject the authority of the Church. God designed us to be one.

33,000 Versions of One

In late June 2007, Pope Benedict XVI issued a statement about the unity of the Church. The Pope reiterated that God has just one Church and that the fullness of Jesus resides only in the Catholic Church. Pope Benedict says these things because the Catholic Church alone stands in the line of Peter, with apostolic succession, and therefore also has the real presence of Christ in the Eucharist. Other Christian groups may offer grace and salvation, but only the Catholic Church houses the fullness of Christ.

When this statement came out, my phone began to ring with calls from my Protestant friends. The questions centered around the same themes:

"How in the world could the Pope proclaim that there is but one, holy, catholic apostolic Church?"

"Why would the Pope say that Protestant groups were not churches but rather 'ecclesial communities'?"

"Is the Pope saying that we are not Christians?"

When you live in a world with 33,000 different permutations of Protestant Christianity, you grow accustomed to spiritualizing every description of the body of Christ. Obviously you cannot sincerely believe that Jesus meant we would *really* be one.

As a Protestant, you just assume that unity is a fairy tale, something God hopes for but does not really mean or expect.

When your churches divide and split and find new ways to disagree on a daily basis, you become accustomed to a model based on group pride, epitomized by conflict, and then followed by division. The Church is reduced to an elective based on what you think, feel, and like. Worse, the Church is optional. Pick what you like or select none at all if you so choose. You can always just find other Christians who believe like you do and begin your own congregation.

Neither popular opinion (where enough people choose to select their own doctrine or structure) nor division are the models of the Church found in Scripture or in the first 1500 years of the Church. *"For all of you are one in Christ Jesus."*

Jesus really did mean it when He said that we would be one body. A body is a very physical metaphor, and the Church really *is* a body.

God's Church consists of more than a group of people who merely decide to meet together because they share similar beliefs or interests. Scripture describes the Church with a very real physical element or dimension.

The Church is the *bride* of Christ.

The Church is the *family* of God.

The Church is the *body* of Christ.

These images are real and tangible because the Church bodily represents Jesus after His Incarnation. It is not just a spiritual entity. The Church has a physical, bodily form.

Just as God is One in Himself and in the Trinity, so too is the Church one in a real, tangible sense. Jesus prayed for His people to be one as God is One. The Church embodies that Oneness.

To embrace splinters and factions as normal, and to call acceptable the 33,000 strains of Christianity diminishes the Church. To baptize division as good means that we reject Jesus' own prayer for us to be one. We weaken the mission of the Church by presenting confusion and chaos to the world.

I discovered the oneness of His body in my Catholic vacation worship experiences. Whether in Seattle with friends, or in Lakeland, Florida, with my mother, I would usually attend a Catholic church when our family was away from home.

When I did so, I experienced the same readings, the same liturgy, the same faith, and the same creed. I shared in the same Eucharist in every setting, whether in America or Europe or Asia. The Mass expresses and demonstrates the oneness of the Church. It is not every congregation making it up for itself. It is the one Church, standing on the foundation of the twelve apostles, sharing the real presence of Christ in the Eucharist.

My daughter, SarahAnn, discovered the very same thing when she left for college. For the first time in her life, she had the freedom to select when, where, and how she desired to worship. For the first time, her father would not be her pastor. This was a pregnant moment for her. Choosing her own faith destiny.

After sampling many Protestant worship experiences on and off campus, a friend in her dorm invited SarahAnn to go to Mass on campus. It is amazing what friendship can bring when we extend an invitation or a kind word. For SarahAnn, like in my own experience with Father Steven, the power of friendship and a simple invitation proved to be life-changing.

Knowing that I was transitioning to become Catholic, SarahAnn decided to attend Mass for herself to see what it was all about. Immediately, as she heard the readings and the liturgy, an "Ah-ha" moment clicked in her spirit and mind.

"Dad's doing the exact same thing in Atlanta that I'm doing here at school. And believers in Johannesburg and Sydney and Dublin are celebrating the same Mass with the same readings and the same Eucharist in the same way. The Church really is one as God is One."

She instantly got it and saw the power of oneness.

That oneness overwhelmed her in direct juxtaposition to the experience of "shopping" for a new church home at college. Instead of trying to find a church she "liked," or one where people agreed with her, the goal came to be becoming a part of God's one Church. There is but one Church home.

The Eucharist unifies us. One body and one cup of blessing. One Savior. There is one altar in His one Church in which the real presence of that Savior is presented to His people.

Once the focus is moved from that altar, and once the real presence of Christ is removed, there is and can be no unity. His presence is real. The real presence binds the Church together. There is no substitute. By that real presence, His body, the Church, coheres.

When our radio ministry began, my sense of the Church's lack of oneness became very pronounced. Many of the people that I interacted with found all the divisions and all the strains of Christianity very confusing. They put it very simply for me. "If Jesus is the way, the truth, and the life, then why do His people suffer from so much division, and so many differences? I am looking for life, and all I find is strife."

These are real questions asked by real people trying to meet God. Through those conversations with
men and women completely disconnected from the
Church, God spoke to me. The same conversation
recurred over and over: "I want to find my way home,
but you all sure make it hard. You can't even agree
on anything. You can't agree on what's happening in
communion. You can't agree on how much water to
use at baptism. You can't agree on what kind of music
to sing. You can't agree on whether men or women
can be pastors. You can't agree on how many books
are in the Bible. You argue with each other. You use
such hateful language towards each other. All I want
is a drink of water. I did not ask for a tsunami from a
fire hydrant. And that is what this feels like."

I felt very ashamed. Shame on us. People are miss-
ing life because of us and our division. Our inability
to be one shortchanges God, and it shortchanges the
world.

Again, I returned to the fundamental question. "If
I am a Protestant, what am I protesting?"

Finally, I remembered my seminary professor's
professed passion for unity and my own questions of
what really binds us believers together. The answer
was obvious. The problem was not the Church; the
problem was me.

"Protesting" reflected my own pride, my own desires, and my own spirit of dissension more than
anything else. The answer was The Church. It already
existed, and I merely needed to come home to it.

By coming home, I could add one small step for
unity in God's people.

Front Porch to the World

A month after Benedict XVI visited America in April 2008, my family, some friends, and I went to the Vatican to do the normal tourist and pilgrimage activities. St. Peter's Basilica. Sistine Chapel. Vatican Museum. San Clemente. A trip to Pompeii.

Since it is customary on Wednesdays, when the Pope is in Rome, for him to share a teaching with all who are gathered in St. Peter's Square, we planned to experience that unique moment.

We arrived early in order to be as near the front as possible. The Pope's chair sat beneath a canopy, sections were cordoned off, and the security forces were in full display. When we arrived, believers had already begun to gather in St. Peter's Square at the entrance to St. Peter's Basilica, built over the tomb of Peter. All in all, 20,000 people gathered that day just to hear a thirty minute message from the Holy Father, the leader of the One Church.

As we waited for the Pope to arrive, the crowds gathered. Groups and individuals from Asia, Africa, South America, and the United States. Pilgrims from all across Europe. Bands of religious sisters adorned in their defining garb. School children from around Italy. Collections of religious brothers, praying the rosary in anticipation of the Pope's appearance and teaching.

A dozen recently married couples sat near the canopy knowing they would receive a personal blessing from the Pope after his words of instruction and inspiration. The brides wore their wedding gowns, and the grooms their tuxedos.

Sheer beauty abounded.

Choirs sang. Banners flew. Chants melodiously hung in the air. The Holy Spirit saturated the front porch of the Church like a mist as people from every race, nation, and tongue gathered for one sacred purpose.

Before my very eyes, the world was gathering as one to worship Christ. We gathered as His one Body. One global, divine family.

I realized that this is the front porch of the Church. Actually, as I looked around, I discovered that this is the front porch of the entire *world*.

Right there on the front porch of the Church, I found a hidden treasure of one. Oneness.

One holy, catholic, apostolic Church.

The Holy Spirit overwhelmed me at that moment.

Here I was, just a few months after my conversion on the Feast of the Epiphany, sitting in the middle of 20,000 fellow pilgrims on the front porch of the world.

It had taken years, but now I was there.

As the one Church, we shared the same Lord, the same Eucharist, the same Holy Father, and the same Blessed Mother. We really were one family. And now we had gathered on the front porch of the old house.

A number of years ago, a Dominican sister politely asked me, "Allen why aren't you a part of the Church?" Now, I am.

"Everything you need is in this house."

CONCLUSION

How do you know when you are home? The streets told me.

Pope Benedict XVI made his first papal visit to America in April, 2008. Deep down inside, I knew I simply had to go. Not so much to see the Holy Father but simply to experience fellow believers all coming together as one.

Something just told me I would experience God's grace - the Holy Spirit prompting me to go.

Through a friend, I received an invitation to the Italian embassy, which was throwing a birthday party for the Pope. The Pope celebrated his birthday while here in America, and a number of groups organized parties. As a new convert, I had high (unrealistic) hopes of meeting the Pope in the greeting line at the embassy for five seconds, to share how delighted I was to have come home to the Church and to thank the Pope for his leadership and example.

On Wednesday morning, I awoke early and began to do some work in the library of the Dominican House of Studies where I was staying with my friend, Father Steven. That afternoon, I called Steven to learn how and where we would rendezvous to head toward the Italian embassy for the party.

The entire section of Washington near Catholic University, and the National Basilica and Shrine, had been shut down because of Pope Benedict's arrival. For security purposes, the streets had been closed for at least a mile in each direction. The Pope was scheduled to come that afternoon to the shrine to meet and celebrate Mass with the Catholic bishops of America.

There would be no public audience. Security was tight in the streets all over Washington as crowds lined the route leading from downtown out to the basilica, throngs hoping to catch a glimpse of the Holy Father and his motorcade as they passed by.

Father Steven explained to me that he was downtown and could not physically get back to the Dominican House of Studies (DHS) because of the security presence. Access to the DHS no longer existed since its building lies directly across the street from the basilica itself. Father Steven could only get within a mile or so from where I was. We would meet in a parking lot near where the blockade began, so I needed to walk out of the quarantined security section to walk toward the area where Father Steven was waiting.

After a shower, I got dressed and left. The entire DHS was empty. I was perplexed at being the only human being around. My mind did not fully comprehend the magnitude of this papal visit. An entire quadrant of Washington had been vacated, all the Dominican priests and staff at the DHS had left to prepare for the visit, and I briskly moved along the corridors, completely oblivious to what I was about to see.

As I walked out the front door of the Dominican House of Studies about an hour before the Holy Father was going to arrive to meet with the bishops, I swam into a wave of people.

The streets around Catholic University teemed with people walking, chanting, singing, and waving banners in every language. People from every race and every tribe mingled on the street in hopes of possibly catching a glimpse of the Pope. Hordes of people, like a great migratory pattern of birds, moved through the streets of our nation's capital.

Palpable electricity filled the air. Street vendors hawked hot dogs, drinks, papal t-shirts, and souvenirs. Children and teenagers sang and chanted; choirs spontaneously performed on the side of the streets. An impromptu, fully disorganized worship experience unfolded as the young and the old, Asian and American, black and white, male and female, all made their way toward the basilica, greeting one another with warm hugs and smiles even though they have never met before. A remarkable oneness crested around me; in fact, it enveloped me as Catholics from every imaginable strain of humanity all gathered together to offer encouragement and love for their Lord and for the Pope. An outpouring of love and hope in the streets of Washington as the people of God migrated toward the National Basilica and Shrine.

Because I was trying to get out of the quarantined area to meet Father Steven, my path forced me to travel against the flowing tide of pilgrims. A lone salmon swimming upstream against a steady current of humans making their way in the opposite direction. Everyone else trying to come *in* to the area as I was working to get *out*. A rushing tide of the worshipers washed over me like a mammoth tidal wave of faith. I swam against the current. Their joy and excitement flowed over me. The energy was, in a single word, exhilarating.

This is the moment I had been waiting for. I was now fully a part of the Church. No need for apologies or embarrassment. The years of journey had culminated in the Holy Spirit's presence all around me on the streets of Washington.

I did not get to meet the Pope that day. But I did get to meet something even more powerful.

Bodies all around me. Bouncing like a pinball, I knew. Here is the one Church, and I am right in the middle of it. Literally. Right there all around me swarmed the Oneness of God and His people, the Church

"Everything you need is in this house."

Welcome home.

APPENDIX:
REAL LIFE HELPS

3
REAL-LIFE
WAYS TO EXPERIENCE
THE POWER
OF
THE EUCHARIST

Select one of these three choices
to grow deeper in love with the Eucharist

1

Meditate on Salvador Dali's painting of the Last Supper.

Salvador Dali's representation of the Last Supper hangs on my office wall and captures my attention several times a day. In the painting, Dali points toward the mystery of the Eucharist and its unique power for believers. At first, I merely thought it was a marvelous and creative rendering of the Last Supper. Over time, this painting has come to represent what I cannot put into words.

Spend some time gazing on this piece of art. You can find it online or purchase a reprint to place in your own special place of reflection. Allow God to shape your soul. Contemplate the mystery of the Eucharist. Meditate on the self-giving love of Jesus our Lord.

2

Read Peter Kreeft's excellent little book on the faith and the Eucharist, *Jesus Shock*.

Enjoy this very clear, very concise book to deepen your experience of the Eucharist. I have recommended it to thousands of people (really!), and have gotten more positive feedback on this short book than on any other. It will inspire you.

3

Visit a chapel near you for Adoration of the Blessed Sacrament.

Sit quietly for one hour in the presence of the Lord who comes to us in the Eucharist. Pray God will use the time to draw you into His heart in the Eucharist. Be transformed.

3
REAL-LIFE WAYS
TO GROW FORWARD
IN HOLINESS

Select one of these three choices
to move toward your destiny

1

Take a one-day retreat.

Your church or diocese probably offers a retreat every month or every year. If not, a nearby monastery is likely to do so. Take advantage of the Church's deep reservoir of holiness by spending a day in a spiritual setting in full silence. If possible, meet with a spiritual director for an hour just to gain outside perspective on your journey toward your destiny: holiness in the image of Jesus. A one day investment will yield results for the whole year.

Attend Mass 7 days in a row.

Look at your calendar right now. Find a week where you can attend the daily Mass at your parish or one near your workplace. Select the time you are most likely to attend. Place it on your calendar now. As you attend Mass each day of that week, go with anticipation for the Lord's holy sacrifice on the altar. You will be meeting your Lord there. Holiness awaits!

3

Read John Paul the Great
by Peggy Noonan.

This wonderful book provides an easy-to-read biography of one of the holiest men of the last century. The stories will inspire you and stir your spirit in ways you will never anticipate. It enriched my life and will do the same for yours. I promise.

3
REAL-LIFE WAYS
TO BE LOVED
BY YOUR FAMILY,
THE SAINTS

Select one of these three choices
to meet your spiritual relatives

1

Meditate on the statuary in your parish.

Your parish will have statues, icons, or other artwork representing saints from the Church's history. Take some time and gaze at one of your favorite pieces. Do some reading on that saint. Get to know him or her. Begin to invite that saint to pray with you and for you. Stop and say hello to that saint each time you arrive at church. This saint is cheering for you!

2.

Enjoy the life of
St. Andrew Bobola
or St. Rita of Cascia.

If you have never learned the story of Andrew Bobola or Rita of Cascia, take an hour to do so. Read about one of them on-line or in the book, *The Incorruptibles*, which is discussed in chapter 4. Remember that you are on the same team as they are. What an amazing thing to be connected to people of such courage and stature in Christ!

Make your family tree of spiritual cheerleaders.

Sketch on a piece of paper the people in your life who have inspired your own faith or encouraged you on your journey. Keep that paper with you as a part of your prayer life. As you pray, invite them to pray with you and for you. You will also discover that over time God will add to your list of fellow believers, both alive and deceased, who are a part of your spiritual family of encouragers. Your family tree will remind you that you are not alone.

3
REAL-LIFE WAYS
TO BE AWESTRUCK
BY MYSTERY

Select one of these three choices to overcome the
world's allergy to God's mystery

1

Make a pilgrimage to the shrines at Lourdes (France) and Fatima (Portugal).

These two holy places will do wonders for your soul. Many groups offer pilgrimages to these holy sites. Hear the stories of miracles, and meet other pilgrims whose lives are being transformed. Invite God to reveal Himself to you in new ways.

Read The Incorruptibles by Joan Carrol Cruz.

Read this inspiring book and delight in how God has preserved in a life-like state the bodies of so many Catholic saints, like Andrew Bobola and Rita of Cascia. The author provides accounts of dozens of the faithful whose bodies still appear almost life-like, and she shows how this phenomenon has never occurred elsewhere in history. The Church is part of God's mystery. Ponder the mystery of our God who preserves some of His saints for our benefit. Their preservation reminds us of His wondrous power not just to make us holy but also to vanquish death. Our God is not confined by the laws of science or of the world.

3

Fast for 24 hours.

Fasting is one of the least used, but most significant, spiritual tools God gives us. If you have never fasted for a full day, try it (unless your doctor advises against it for medical reasons). Very few Americans have encountered the face of God simply by living on water for a full day. Each time I teach a group about fasting, I meet people who are afraid of the very idea of living a single day without food. Trust God. Speak to your priest if you have questions. No one can fully explain how the experience deepens you, only that it does. Each time you feel a pang of hunger, use that moment for prayer to invite the Holy Spirit to invade your life. You will meet the mystery of God.

3
REAL-LIFE WAYS
TO EMBRACE
THE AUTHORITY OF
THE CHURCH

Select one of these three choices to appreciate the gift
of God's Church in your life

1

Read the Catechism.

Seriously. I mean it. Actually sit down and read the Catechism. Take your time.

Make notes on the pages to remember questions you have. Underline parts that fascinate you. Discuss interesting portions with your spouse or close friends. Rejoice in being a part of a Church who has pondered the Truth of Jesus Christ for more than two millennia. When you have completed the reading, make time to meet with a priest to discuss what you have learned and what questions you have. Over time, God will draw you into the Truth in a fresh and powerful way.

2

Share in a Catholics Come Home class or in RCIA as a student or sponsor.

Discover the truths of the faith in your own parish. Enroll in a Catholics Come Home class if your parish offers one. Or if you have never been in RCIA, make the time to do so in order to learn about the doctrines of the faith. If you are already confirmed, re-discover your faith by serving as a sponsor of someone else. The journey will enrich your life and ground you in the Truth.

3

Invite your family or friends to join you for a day of service in a soup kitchen or a homeless shelter.

As you serve the poor, your mind and understanding will be transformed. It is important to balance your mind with your hands as you discover the Truth of the faith in a new way. Believers are doers and not just hearers of the Word of Truth.

3
REAL-LIFE WAYS
TO EXPERIENCE THE
POWER OF ONE

Select one of these three choices to grow in unity with
God's global family, the Church

1

If you are a Protestant, examine what are you protesting.

Martin Luther, John Calvin, and King Henry broke with the Church for reasons that were very important to them. Their decisions broke the unity of the one catholic, apostolic, and holy Church. Since then, Protestants have fractured into more than 33,000 branches and streams of the faith. Examine your own life. Do some reading about beliefs. Take a moment to decide whether you have a really good reason to be separated from the One true Church that Jesus desired for us in His prayer in John 17.

2

Make a Vatican pilgrimage.

Visit the front porch of the Church for yourself. Examine the treasures of the Church that reside in Rome and the Vatican. Visit St. Peter's Basilica and the Sistine Chapel. Watch as pilgrims from every corner of the world come together as one. Bask in that unity. And if you have a moment, visit the church at San Clemente which possesses the oldest baptismal pool in existence. It is inspiring to stand in unity with the believers who came before us. If your budget cannot allow such a pilgrimage, take advantage of the virtual tours of these sites offered online.

3

Attend Mass in multiple settings and enjoy the sameness.

When you vacation or visit family or friends in different cities, towns, or countries, make an effort to attend Mass in each new location. Your heart will find comfort in the familiar liturgy and rhythm of the Mass regardless of the language being spoken. You can even experience new dimensions of the sameness of the Mass by visiting various parishes in your own diocese to sense the power of one. The same creed. The same Eucharist. The same altar. The same words of consecration. One holy catholic and apostolic Church.

ACKNOWLEDGMENTS

By God's grace, I am the richest man in the world. He has filled my life with good people, good family, and good friends. Each of those has made this work possible in some way. And I am deeply grateful:

To Anita, SarahAnn, and Griffin. I love you more than meat loves salt.

To Christina Reinsel, whose hard work in transcribing made this possible.

To Gigi Devanney, for her editing and proofreading gifts. (Go Dreadnaughts!)

To Matthew Kelly and Pat Lencioni, who have welcomed me as a brother and whose friendship has nurtured this work.

To Father Steven Boguslawski, O.P., and the St. Joseph Province of the Dominican Order of Preachers. They have inspired this book in more ways than can be named.

To the priests of the Archdiocese of Atlanta. Monsignor Joe Corbett, Monsignor Paul Reynolds, Monsignor Henry Gracz, and Father David Dye in particular.

To the Dominican Sisters at Our Lady of Grace Monastery in North Guilford, Connecticut. Your prayers have made all the difference.

To Glenn, Hollyce, Doug, Dianne, Stan, and Kay, whose gracious and generous support has made new things possible.

To Andy Borgmann, the Wonder Boy.

ABOUT THE AUTHOR

Allen Hunt and his team are pursuing a vision to build a nationwide talk radio show on mainstream stations to create a place where real life and faith come together. The Allen Hunt Show focuses *not on what's right and left but on what's right and wrong.* Already syndicated on stations around the country each weekend, the show became a Monday-Friday weeknight show, beginning September 7, 2009. The weeknight show has rapidly grown to stations nationwide.

Allen's diverse interests in sports, history, business, politics, and culture intersect with faith in a creative and refreshing way, providing a unique view of life. Such a view makes for compelling and engaging talk radio.

Allen has been named to Talkers Magazine's prestigious list of the 100 heavy hitters in talk radio, receiving a ranking unprecedented for a newcomer in the industry. His weekly real life and faith columns can now be found at www.townhall.com.

Allen stepped aside July 1, 2007, as Senior Minister at Mount Pisgah, a United Methodist congregation serving more than 15,000 persons each week through all of its ministries in Alpharetta, Georgia. While at Mount Pisgah, Allen helped to develop comprehensive ministries with children and students as well as a Christian school with over 1200 students, only the second Methodist-church related comprehensive school in the nation; a Beacon of

Hope pregnancy resource center; and the Summit Counseling Center. Mount Pisgah, with a desire to be a People of Compassion, is known for its leadership in serving the poor and the forgotten in our culture through ministries with the homeless, those in crisis, and those in need. Mount Pisgah also multiplies its ministry with key dynamic ministry partners on each continent of the globe. This powerful combination of ministries made Mount Pisgah one of the largest Methodist congregations in the world.

Prior to full-time ministry, Allen worked in management consulting with Kurt Salmon Associates, an international leader in the textile, apparel, and retail industries. Allen grew up in Brevard, North Carolina, and Lakeland, Florida. He was then educated at Mercer (B.B.A.) and Emory (M.Div.) Universities, before earning a Ph.D. in New Testament and Ancient Christian Origins from Yale University. He has taught and preached in Catholic, Methodist, Baptist, and non-denominational congregations, colleges, and seminaries.

Before entering the ministry, Allen wandered away from God's plans for his life. Allen quickly discovered that a life serving himself, his own pleasures, and his own plans did not result in much. One day, while entering a Wall Street high-rise in New York, Allen stepped over a homeless man huddled on a subway grating for warmth. At that pivotal moment, God taught Allen that it was time to leave behind his own plans and embrace God's plans for his life. A life of serving others and following Jesus. Allen then became an ordained pastor.

On January 6, 2008, on the Feast of the Epiphany, Allen converted to Catholicism. This transition represented the culmination of a 15 year journey in which God began leading Allen home to the Church. In many ways, this transition was effected by the prayers of a group of Dominican sisters at Our Lady of Grace in North Guilford, Connecticut, who have been praying for Allen since he shared lectures with them during the season of Lent in 1992. Allen's home parish is in Norcross, Georgia.

Allen and his wife, Anita, have two daughters, SarahAnn and Griffin Elizabeth, both of whom are grown and working on fun ventures. Sadly, that leaves Allen and Anita as empty nesters!

the **allen hunt** show

it's not about right or left, it's about right or wrong.

YOU ARE INVITED!

Be a member of the
Allen Hunt Show Email Family

Allen would love to hear from you
And as a part of his email family,
you will receive a weekly email from Allen

Inspiring
Helpful
Timely
Free

And you will be the first to know about Allen's
upcoming speaking engagements, newest
books, and schedule of guided travels

Sign up now for free at
http://family.allenhuntshow.com